Mount Everest and Mount Kilimanjaro

Seven Mountain Story
Book I

Walter Glover, MTS

Advance Praise

"Faith, hope, and love fuel this mountain climber's passion to reach new heights."   —North Vernon Plain-Dealer
The Criterion, Indianapolis

"Walter's treks are inspiring to many people. It's not just the challenge of the climb at his age when most people are slowing down, but it's where his heart is while making the difficult grades."
—Bedford Times Mail editorial

"Glover meshes with fitness as he does with prayer. He trains 120 miles per month, not simply walking or jogging but climbing any and every hill he can find while carrying a 40-pound backpack and wearing boots. One mile a day must be vertical, by the way."
—Dale Moss
The Louisville (KY) Courier-Journal

"Glover has combined his passion for mountains with another passion, helping people, youth in particular. His expeditions to hike mountains in foreign lands are dubbed 2Trek4Kids.
—Leader-Democrat

"Wally Glover of St. Vincent's Jennings Hospital in Indiana, won the first national Eye on Wellness" award from Virgin Health Miles. Wally is an active 61-year old HealthMiles member, committed to staying active and promoting activity within his community.
—Virgin Pulse
Health Miles

"Glover goes to schools and tells students the rewards of getting naturally high and healthy. He tells them they can do whatever their heartfelt passion pictures.
—The Columbus Republic

"Overcoming the mountainous battle of knocking down childhood obesity will take more than one man on a mission—it's going to take a change in society and its behaviors. However, thanks to people like Glover who point their commitment toward doing good, we know we're taking positive steps in the right direction."

—Bedford Times Mail editorial

NorLightsPress.com
762 State Road 458
Bedford IN 47421

Printed in the United States of America
ISBN: 978-0-9964559-7-8

Cover Design by Vorris "Dee" Justesen
Book Design by Nadene Carter
Edited by Sammie Justesen

First printing, 2016

"How beautiful on the mountain are the feet..."
Isaiah 52:7

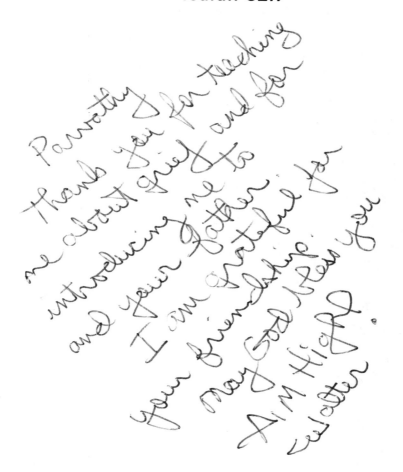

Dorothy

Thanks you for teaching
me about grief and for
introducing me to
and your father.
I am grateful for
your friendship.

May God bless you

Aim High

Walter

Dedication

To my Godmother Aunt Angie Meno,
Lori Walton,
Siena, Dominic, and Kathryn Glover, and
Drew, Andrew, and Jill Glover.

My you find peace & comfort
as you journey through life.
My thoughts will always be
with you & know you are loved.
Mary

Contents

Mount Everest Highlight

"*P*raise the Lord!" –an expression for this day, and also an act. I am out of bed by 5:30 a.m., and dang it's cold in my tiny room. The door is only a few feet beyond my bed and twin beds are wedged into this narrow space, with maybe two feet separating them. Each bed includes about a yard of storage space between the foot of the bed and the wall with the door. On the other end the beds are shoved up beside a poorly sealed window that lets cold air in. Hooks on the wall for hanging coats and clothes complete the Spartan amenities. I wonder if the other occupant of my room–a mouse behind the wall, considered his quarters cramped as he scrambled about behind the thin walls during the night.

Beyond my door is a short hallway leading to the community loo and an adjoining common area. We're sleeping indoors, but it's cold; very cold. Any heat we get comes from a fireplace in the common area, but there is no heat that I can discern. The thin exterior walls that barely protect us from the weather admit the cold, and perhaps the mice. The small window is a sieve for cold. Oh, well. I slept soundly and awakened at sunrise, as intended. I have plans before we push off on our day's trek.

The first thing I do is read some scripture by flashlight before leaving my warm sleeping bag. I'm already wearing polypropylene bottoms and top with warm socks and one layer of trekking clothes. When I stir from my cocoon sleeping bag I need only a few quick minutes to get dressed. I'm eager to get outside, wishing to take in the Himalayan range at sunrise, with a setting full moon gloriously shining above the tallest peaks on the planet. I intend to see the greater light, the sun, and the lesser light, the moon. I am expectant to see Chomolungma, Mother Goddess of Earth, while the mountain and I occupy the same area of the third planet, Earth. Then I will visit the monastery for morning worship, as I discussed yesterday with the monk.

Out of my room, I part the insulating doorway blankets aside, and push open the heavy wood door of our monastery grounds' lodge. Am I the only one outside just now? Well, my "community" this morning is nature. And nature is vividly present in its full regalia, soundless and richly stunning.

The morning moon hangs high over the left side of the mountain range, luminous and bright, nearly full as I behold its setting. It is white above white, the circular and cratered moon above the jagged mountains covered in their white mantle of glaciers and permanent snowfields. I am so transfixed I realize I forgot the greater light—the sun. I turn 180 degrees to see it. Whoa! I cannot yet see the sun's full orb. Instead, I see its dazzling rays radiating over the top of a mountain between us. The mountain is so tall it still has the planet eclipsed. I stand in the mountain's shade. Yet when I turn back to look again at the Himalaya, sunlight reaches the moon and the mountains. The sky is brilliantly blue, bluer than at home. I wonder if that's because we are at 12,600 feet and the air is thinner than southern Indiana's 600 feet of elevation. I hope my camera will record the true blueness as I see it so vividly.

After meditating on the creative majesty of Elohim, "Creator God" in Hebrew, I walk to the monastery for morning worship. As noted by the monk, a trumpet sound comes from the monastery to break the silence of dawn. I expect this has been happening for a hundred some years, which reminds me to check the monastery's founding date. Yesterday the courtyard bustled with foreign trekkers going to worship, but at this hour it is empty. Well, there is a sacred cow in the courtyard, plus a dog. I admit myself through the ornate door, as I did yesterday, remembering to take off my boots. Brrrr! The stone floor is freezing cold.

Prayer already is under way—I hear chanting. I follow my steps of yesterday, hoping to sit where I did before. I smile, thinking there are people like me in every church who think their pew is *their pew* and get offended if someone else takes that seat." Well, "my seat" is wide open, close to the altar and all its man-made beauty. I am the only person who looks like me in attendance. This doesn't surprise me when I think about it. I am probably the only member of the trekker / climber community who has seminary experience and some feel for how a monastery operates. No one else knows or wishes to be here at sunrise unless they wear the purple and yellow robe of a monk.

Well, not to dwell on that. I am here for the sacred worship, for prayer, for praise of God and gratitude to him as I know him, and to respect the monastics before me who know him as they do. Our practice and our understanding may look and seem different. Yet, I agree with one of my teachers who said, "There's more that unites we people of faith than what separates us. Concentrate on what unites us rather than what separates us."

And so I listen to their words, which I don't understand. I observe their rituals, which I don't understand. What I understand is the reverence in how they conduct themselves this morning. I understand how important peace is to them, and how importantly they regard life. I understand how they, like Jewish families the world over, were run out of their homeland. In Tibet, hundreds of Buddhist monasteries were destroyed and thousands of monks and Tibetans killed by Chinese invaders about the time I was born. I marvel at this sacred place man has built, and rebuilt, and rebuilt again. I marvel at the setting in this extraordinary environment where the temple is located, perhaps more beautiful because it is so arduous to reach. I admire how these men have given themselves to God. And I offer my prayers with theirs, knowing that where two or more are gathered, we are promised God is present in their midst.

After some time in community worship, I stand, bow, and quietly excuse myself. I place some rupees in the collection box, put on my (now cold) trek boots, and thank God for His place at the center of my life. I also thank Him for this faith community and that I was part of it for a while.

I leave the monastery feeling vibrant and alive, although walking on chilly feet. I worshipped this morning in the great natural cathedral of the Himalayan Mountains with God's magnificent nature surrounding me, and then I worshipped within a man-made structure with a community that is rich in peace, in tradition, in faith. Talk about vibrant and alive.

Foreword

*C*limbing the highest mountains on each of the seven continents was not an ambition born of my childhood dreams. I was five years old when Sir Edmund Hillary and Tenzing Norgay became the first summiteers of Mount Everest. I was 30 before I saw the mountains of Colorado. In the 1950s, those of us who lived amid the hot, humid cornfields of Indiana didn't hold much regard for mountain ranges in the American West, let alone peaks in a far off land called Nepal. So the question of why I was drawn to mountain tops is a good one. Do you believe in voices? Well, I heard a voice distinctly calling me to the mountains. Maybe it was John Muir; maybe someone else. Muir is often quoted: "The mountains are calling and I must go." Well, someone told me, "Go!" I heard the voice and went.

My response to that call is one reason for this book.

A second reason is that climbing mountains became a gateway to support a cause that is dear to my heart: youth obesity prevention and treatment programs. Why I was drawn to this issue has a down-to-earth Hoosier answer. As I worked in the hospital system as a chaplain, I came to see that Indiana has a major problem with obesity—especially childhood obesity. And the three southern Indiana communities where I ministered for St. Vincent Hospitals had way too much evidence of this, ranging from teen-agers to much younger boys and girls. I watched a quiet epidemic undermine our youth. Knowing an answer, was available, I acted. You see, I grew up with the answer.

My Aunt Angie, who was my Godmother and helped raise my brother and I, was overweight as a child. She wanted no part of obesity as an adult. Her name was Angie Meno and she was eating healthy as early as the 1950s, decades before everyone else caught on. She also played tennis and golf, walked, swam, and used indoor exercise equipment at home. Aunt Angie was even active on her 95th birthday. That day, while an at-home hospice patient, Angie played both golf and tennis. From childhood I learned about nutrition and exercise from Angie, so working with overweight kids was second nature for me. Helping these children in the communities of southern Indiana, where I grew up, was the right thing to do.

Fortunately, a bright, energetic RN at St. Vincent Hospitals shared Angie's passion for wellness through exercise, nutrition, and education. This woman co-developed a scientifically-based way to help kids lose weight—and keep it off. After my Everest expedition and before my Mount Kilimanjaro expedition, I found myself heading a fund raising initiative to help children in southern Indiana avoid what my beloved Aunt Angie suffered from. Along the way our clinicians shared my mountain stories with the young patients, some of whom I met. I hope the children gained inspiration from my climbs as a senior citizen.

What follows is the story of how, in the spring of 2005, when elite climbers were gathering in Nepal to climb Everest, I heard a voice calling me there; how I ignored the voice and tried to forget about it. Twelve months later, again during the climbing season at Everest, the voice returned with more urgency, higher volume, and further information. The voice was definitely calling me to Everest. Not to its summit known as the "roof of the world," but to its "porch," if you will. The voice was calling me on a trek to Everest Base Camp. And the voice was not to be denied. I began writing this book in July 2013, having just returned from my second trip to climb Mount Rainier. In between, I visited five major mountains:

- Everest in Nepal,
- Kilimanjaro in Africa,
- Elbrus in Russia,
- Kociuszko in Australia,
- Aconcagua in Argentina,
- and then Rainier for training, with my sights set on McKinley / Denali in Alaska, and the Vinson Massif in Antarctica for a finish.

Minus Rainier, these mountains are collectively known as the Seven Summits—the highest mountains on each of the seven continents. Climbing on them became my adventure quest, which I call *Seven Mountain Story*.

Along the way, more than $130,000 was raised to combat youth obesity. We were able to open and sustain three youth weight management prevention and treatment clinics, one each in North Vernon, Salem, and Bedford, Indiana. The fund-raising efforts met with challenges—some of them surprising, but we did create three successful and sorely needed programs which also knew success. I was the pastoral care chaplain for St. Vincent at the three hospital ministries where the weight management programs operate.

The programs use a medical model to fight one of the most serious issues faced by one in every three Indiana children. Unless addressed, childhood obesity sets up a dismal future that may include diabetes, hypertension, fatty liver disease, orthopedic pain, heart disease, stroke, and cancer. The hospital-based programs help empower children (with their parents and sometimes grandparents) to become adults who know how and why to choose wellness behaviors. The emphasis of the program is to increase knowledge and build behavior management skills so kids will make good choices for nutrition, exercise, and wellness. RNs, dietitians, physical therapists, and behavioral therapists staff the programs. Money is raised by my climbs and dispensed as scholarships, for the most part, so all kids have easy access to the program. As this is written more than 100 children have participated in the program. I pay all my own expedition expenses out of pocket.

Although this book is an adventure story, visiting the mountains was also a spiritual quest. I am always struck by the stark beauty, weather, and elements surrounding the world's highest mountains, and the creative forces that produced them. Glaciers encapsulate many of the peaks and some of these glaciers are in retreat—in some cases because of global warming, and sometimes not because of global warming. The question for mankind, and for me is this: Are we good stewards of the earth and its resources? This, after all, was the first task God bestowed on man: "Take care of the planet." This book will touch on that subject, but don't expect a definitive answer. I am intrigued by how the mountains came about. I appreciate that fundamental science evolved the mountains. But for me, behind that science is the creative energy of Elohim (in Hebrew, Elohim is the word for Creator God).

This isn't a book about science, nor is it a theology textbook. It is simply my story. And part of my story is my theology training and its influence on me as a climber in the mountain environment. Thus, threaded throughout, you will find Godly references and connections. And you will read of how my faith serves me, and me it. Mountain literature makes for powerful reading. Not many people hope to climb the Seven Summits. Fewer write about it. Even fewer mountain books concern themselves with the spirituality of mountains.

In the pages ahead you will meet Lori Walton, my life partner, who was the central figure bringing youth weight management programs to southern Indiana St. Vincent hospitals.

Watch for the story of the 21 year old man who climbed Kilimanjaro on holiday with his mother while I was also on that stunning African mountain. He would suffer altitude sickness and die in a hospital in the Tanzanian village where I stayed. Around that same time a man my age who lived an hour from me in Indiana would die in a Kathmandu hospital after becoming gravely ill at Everest Base Camp, where I had been months before. While at Everest I suffered acute mountain sickness and perhaps the beginnings of cerebral edema. Mountains can be unforgiving at times. At other times they are so generous.

And so I begin sharing my stories with you. "Jambo, Jambo!" The word translates from Swahili as "Hello, Hello" spoken enthusiastically. Greetings of hello and welcome to you. Come along—join the expedition!

Walter Glover

SECTION ONE: Mount Everest

1. Mount Everest

*I*n April, 2007, I traveled to Mount Everest where I would trek to its base camp at 17,600 feet—three miles higher than my home in Columbus, Indiana, where the farmers would soon be planting corn and soybeans. Meanwhile, in the Solo Khumbu region of Everest, elite mountaineers of the world were gathering on the mountain's south side in Nepal, and on its north side in Tibet, for the annual climbing season. This year I would be part of that international pilgrimage to the Mecca of mountains.

At the tender age of 59, this was my rookie trip to serious elevation. I did not have interest in visiting all Seven Summits, nor had I considered founding three youth obesity prevention and treatment clinics for St. Vincent Hospitals, using pledge money raised from mountain expeditions. I had not yet graduated to altruistic adventure. The Everest trip was unadulterated adventure for me alone.

I'd been studying Mt. Everest for several years, fascinated by the goings on there. The climbing season in the Himalayas happened in March, April, and May, before the annual monsoons from India arrived to create mega snowfalls. During the climbing months I followed the Everest adventures by computer. A website, everestnews.com, provided daily reports from climbers who relayed info by sat phones—satellite telephones. Those digital images and words from Everest captivated me.

And ultimately it happened—a mystical, digital-age electronic calling lured me from behind the laptop screen of vicarious adventure to the real experience. I spent much of April and May 2007, in Nepal, bound for Everest Base Camp. As I set out on a guided trek with other adventure seekers, I also looked forward to the spiritual dimension to this adventure. After all we'd be at Tengboche Monastery, a sacred Tibetan Buddhist center in the heart of the Himalayan Solo Khumbu. The Buddhists believe God resides on the mountain.

Beyond wishing to get close to God in Nepal, one of my prayers included a hope for human diversity among the people I would meet. The majesty of nature created by Elohim at Genesis time would speak to me every day, I realized. I was certain the physical toil would test the stamina that allowed me to complete 50 mini-marathons, combined with bicycling 60,000 miles in nine consecutive years.

However, I did not know the toll aloneness would have on me. Loneliness plagued me. Being away from my sons and their wives, my friends, and my hospital ministry for almost a month created emotions I didn't anticipate. Yet, I was traveling to Everest, the Roof of the World. As the mountain books and guides reminded me: "Only one percent of the world's population are able to experience such adventure."

This chapter and the remainder of the book will allow you to share my first two expeditions, divided into days or blocs of calendar time. The journals I kept at each mountain are the principal sources for this writing.

Friday, 27 April, 2007

My plane arrived in Kathmandu, but alas, my luggage remained at Los Angeles International Airport. Storms in the Midwest delayed and rerouted many flights, and I almost missed my Bangkok connection from Los Angeles. Hence, my luggage was an ocean and more behind me as I boarded the plane for Kathmandu. I would find this out later. For now, ignorance is bliss. All I had were the clothes on my back and a book bag. During the plane's approach into Kathmandu from Bangkok, one look from my cabin window connected me to my roots and to my future.

The jet engine on the wing outside my porthole window was stamped Rolls Royce. This meant it was probably manufactured at the Rolls plant in Indianapolis, an hour north of my home. I thought of people I know who worked there. Then I thought of St. Vincent Hospital in Indianapolis, where I worked for eight years as I trained to be a hospital pastoral care chaplain. Looking beyond the plane's wingtip out into the blue sky, I kept my eyes on alert. I arranged to be on this side of the plane for a reason—and soon my patience was rewarded: There they were! In the distance, white pinnacles pierced the cloud deck and I saw Mount Everest and its neighbors. I whispered, "Oh, my God!" The work of Elohim (Hebrew for the Creator God). Everest's shoulders and peak rose above the clouds. What an awesome and awe-filling sight. Our pilots were humming those Rolls Royce engines, cruising at 30,000 feet, a thousand or so feet above the height of Everest. I laughed, telling myself, "Enjoy this view now, because next time you see it, you'll be looking up—way up—at the mountain, and toiling uphill on foot."

Our flight from Bangkok landed at Kathmandu. The first two people I met on the ground were Jewish; one of them on my expedition and the second on another Everest expedition. During my flights I met and had a cordial conversation with Tenzing, who identified himself as head of the Tibetan community in Denver. Tenzing was a Nepalese man whose family owned a tea house, or lodge, at Namche Bazaar, a kind of "capitol" city on the way to Everest. Later I would meet his family at Namche. I also met Bob, the brother of the youngest Canadian to summit Everest. Two days from home and already an expedition prayer request was answered—my prayer for diversity in the people I met.

I was a little stern with Thai Airways when I realized my bags were missing, especially after learning the plane from Bangkok to Kathmandu only arrived every other day. I felt a surge of panic, realizing I wouldn't see my luggage until late afternoon on the day before leaving for Everest. My first response was a new prayer: "Dear God, please let them get here. All my trek gear is in that bag and back pack. Please help!" The downside is, I was curt with the airline agent.

When I checked in at the Shangri-La Hotel, I also expressed anger at Peregrine, my outfitter. This was more frustration than good sense. The liaison officer for the outfitter looked at me and said simply, "Walter, we did not lose your bags." Of course, he was right. Having fumed, stewed, and then prayed, which of course is the incorrect order as prayer should have been first—I let go of it.

"I'm over it," I told myself. There was nothing to be done at that moment. Unless of course I wanted to buy all new gear and hope the travel insurance company would pay for it. I decided to make "F" decisions—to be f-aithful and f-rugal. I would give my prayers a chance.

I had dinner alone at the hotel restaurant and fell into bed, hopeful and jet-lagged, by eight p.m.

Saturday, 28 April, 2007

I had breakfast with Mike, the man I met earlier who was on my expedition, and his son Ben, also making the trek to Base Camp. Then we three toured Thamel and Durbar Square, two well-known tourist marketplace areas of Kathmandu. We also viewed a vast Buddhist Temple containing a huge prayer wheel. This visit stayed on the superficial level and lacked the depth of sacred space spirituality I hoped for. Silly me. Later, I kicked myself when I learned where I was. This was Boudhanath, the largest and most revered Buddhist temple on earth. When you are literally on the outside looking in, you don't get it. I was on the tourist level of visitor. It was my own fault. I hadn't done my homework on Kathmandu. Rats.

In the vast city I saw both squalor and beauty. Blooming trees abounded around the historic temple site. There were also two mothers with babies on their arms begging for money. The scent of incense filled the air. High pressure sellers hawked T-shirts and everything else. The goods seemed way over-priced. Two cows—sacred here—lounged in the street, compromising traffic flow, as evidenced by blaring horns. Feces dotted the sidewalks and by appearance I wondered if they were human, not animal. This was all within a few blocks of the stunning Presidential Palace.

Kathmandu, the capitol of Nepal, is the seat of the Nepali government which is housed within the palace. Not so stunning was the tall iron gate surrounding the palace, with armed sentries posted every block or so. Two soldiers babysat a 50 caliber machine gun above the entry gate. So many things vied for my attention, both blight and beauty. I felt, as some would say, conflicted. Nepalese noise, commotion, and the insane driving in this major world center and capital to the epicenter of mountaineering stole my peace. Kathmandu was frenetic.

Back at the hotel, I needed a nap. People on expedition share rooms, unless one indicates otherwise and pays extra for solitude and space. A knock on the door disrupted my regained exterior and internal quiet. It was an Australian named John came to claim the room's other bed. As he brought in his luggage, I was reminded it would be 24 more hours before, hopefully and God willing please, I would be re-united with my baggage. John was on another Himalayan trekking expedition, the Annapurna circuit.

Dorzee (sounds like door-Gee) would be our sirdar, or expedition leader. We met earlier when I was first frustrated by my MIA bags at the airport. He smiled and seemed friendly—good for starters. I liked him. He convened a meeting of our group, which included nine trekkers and four guides. I was the odd man out in the sense that each of my fellow trekkers had one companion. Deckland and Ingrid, the youngest of our number, were a couple from Australia. Ron and Eddie were married partners from the states. Mike and Ben were the father and son I met. Tom and Trina, widower and widow, were friends who knew each other because, with their late spouses, they were longtime friends as couples. Tom and Trina's friendship continued, although not romantically. I alone was alone.

Dorzee had three guides assisting him: Sailah, Ramish, and Raju. The latter two were young and I had the impression they were being mentored by the two senior guides.

Dorzee hosted a team welcome meeting in a large conference room of our Shangri-La Hotel. We all sat around a large conference table and began by introducing ourselves and sharing background stories. Dorzee also collected travel and personal info from us, and then passed out information from his organization. After this, he did some coaching around what we should expect. It was straight-forward and I heard no surprises. Despite not knowing the Buddhist temple, I earnestly tried to be a good advance student and scout the trek to Base Camp. What I heard confirmed my expectations. Nonetheless, "arduous" summed up the trek and climb before us. This was a big deal; huge really. Yet I felt ready for the challenge—respectfully intimidated and hopeful.

I had trained my butt off to be in the best shape of my life so I could make it to and from Everest Base Camp. My training began in earnest six months earlier in late autumn. A beautiful municipal park is one block from my home, encircled by a one mile-long People Trail. I trekked it every day, carrying a 25 pound backpack and wearing trek boots to simulate conditions on the mountain. For up and down climbing (this was pancake flat Indiana after all), I used steps in another municipal park two miles away with a 98 foot tower. My engineering friends calculated five times up and down this tower would equal approximately one mile. My 20 minute linear mile pace just about corresponded to the up and down pace on the tower. I wanted to average three miles a day minimum in my gear, with one of the miles being vertical. I figured with six months of training I'd be ready. Thus, I trained virtually every day, with week end routes going longer.

I found an Indianapolis-based medical doctor with travel medicine credentials who was familiar with mountains and what elevation does to human physiology. Dr. Jones was most helpful with meds, inoculations, and general mountain physiology advice. I was in great shape, having done the requisite training, and I'd done my homework so nothing Dorzee said in our meeting was a surprise. The loos, or primitive toilets, would be a challenge. What I hadn't fully anticipated was how difficult reaching 17,600 feet of elevation would be. How could I have known? But let me not get ahead of my story.

I shared fully with people at home and during Dorzee's group meeting with the team how I came to be in Kathmandu because the website on Mount Everest whetted my interest. I read it faithfully every day during the climbing season, starting in about 2000. I marveled at the exploits of the climbers, athletes of incomparable skill and endurance. They were the best of the best to be climbing to the top of the world at 29,035 feet.

I began to consume books written about Everest and other mountains. I realized I was becoming a student of the mountains, from afar.

In the spring of 2005, while checking out the everstnews.com website, I heard a voice say, "You know, you could do that." At first blush, not questioning where the voice came from, I thought the voice was suggesting the preposterous idea of climbing Mount Everest. I wasted no time shutting it up and even laughing at it. The voice didn't argue—it simply went still. End of story.

Was I hearing voices? Hmmm. I dismissed it so quickly I didn't ask where it came from or who it was.

The voice disappeared. All remained quiet. Peace was restored after the ludicrous suggestion surfaced momentarily and was sent packing. Ah yes, well . . . Voices with intentions don't easily surrender. The voice was suspended, but it waited.

Fast forward 12 months later into the next Everest climbing season, when I returned to the website. The voice also returned. This time it was louder, more urgent, and provided information. "You know," it said, "You could do that. You could trek to Everest Base Camp." This time I listened and received the full message, because the news was delivered in such a manner I couldn't interrupt. It seemed as if the voice knew how to secure my attention after being rudely rebuffed the previous year.

My simple response was, "Yeah, I *could* do that." My immature and untimely presumption of a year earlier about climbing Everest was misguided. This wasn't about a climb to planet Earth's highest point of 5.5 miles high. It was about a trek to the mountain's "porch," as I nicknamed Everest Base Camp. The Roof of the World was the summit at 29,035. The porch was at 17,600 feet. I would not need the technical mountaineering skills possessed by elite men and women mountaineers from around the world, but to visit the porch of Everest I still needed to be in the best shape of my life.

The next click of my mouse, not because I intended it so, took me to a web site about trekking to Mount Everest Base Camp. First a "voice," and second an unintended link. Had something gone digitally awry? Or was inspiration dawning? That happened in April-May, 2006. Four months later, by Labor Day in September, I was registered for the trip. In between registration and departure, I kicked my own butt with vigorous training.

That night, after Dorzee's meeting, all of us went to a traditional Nepalese restaurant, complete with a cultural troupe of folk dancing girls. The crew began to get acquainted. I ate dinner with the 20-something Aussies, Deckland and Ingrid, whom I began to gently tease as "the kids," because they were younger than my own adult sons. As we sipped a beer and ate, they tried unsuccessfully to teach me about cricket while we watched a match on the restaurant's television.

After dinner we joined the rest of our crew and the other tourist patrons in a mock ceremony conducted by a Hindi troupe of dancers. They danced enthusiastically. Growing more reverent, they next did a kind of anointing of all of us, and poured us a small, powerful drink that I didn't care for the taste of—to seal the deal, I supposed. I wondered if I were converted to another faith tradition as I receive a peel-off red dot to place on my forehead. More diversity, I told myself.

A beverage I drank during dinner agreed with me—a tasty beer aptly named Everest. The bottle label had the photograph of

Tenzing Norgay on the mountain summit, taken by Edward Hillary, the first summiter in 1953. We returned to the Shangri-La and I went to bed with a glow, my lost luggage far from my mind and still far from my body. Somewhere my peel-on dot had dropped off.

Sunday, 29 April, 2007

My belongings (with me) included an abbreviated Bible with the New Testament book of Acts of the Apostles, writings that portray the early Christian church's development. During this first mountain trip I wasn't experienced enough to carry a tiny Bible, but I did know better than to bring a scholar's study Bible in my backpack. I opted for an abridged Biblical book that coincided with the early Christian movement following the Easter resurrection of Christ. As Easter Sunday had just passed, the calendars of church and secular society coincided during my trip. And, importantly on the mountain, my few pages of Acts of the Apostles weighed only a few ounces. Thus, the practical wisdom was good thinking for both a theologian and mountain rookie.

On this Sunday morning, reading Acts in my room at the Shangi-La represented my worship service away from my home. Biblical reading first thing in the morning has been my practice now for the last 20 years. When a church is unavailable on Sunday, my reading is a substitute.

My Australian roommate awakened and headed to the bathroom after giving me a "Good Morning" greeting in English I didn't understand because of his Aussie accent. But I did hear John ask what I was reading. I showed him my Bible.

Upon returning from the can, he picked up a book from his gear, so I returned the favor and asked what he was reading. His words still ring in my ears: "Mr. Mark. Good to start the day with a bit of the Word don't you think? Let's see what Mr. Mark has to say."

I knew John referred to Mark the evangelist, the New Testament second author—after Matthew and before Luke. We both laughed. I like to think God smiled with us, and I remembered the line from Scripture, "Where two or more are gathered in my name . . .".

Our homemade Sunday worship service soon enlarged and diversified as our group went on a Sunday sight-seeing expedition and took in the Hindu Monkey Temple scene. On the previous day I made prayers at the Buddhist temple's huge prayer wheel, tall as a basketball hoop back home. Today I saw a different kind of beauty. This place is called the monkey temple because a grove of trees on the grounds are habitat for a multitude of Kathmandu's monkeys.

Kathmandu is situated in a sub-tropical valley just north of Nepal's frontier with India and offers habitat for many animals we know from zoos. The Monkey Temple, properly called Swayambhunath, is another Buddhist Temple and features holy men revered by their community, wearing long braided hair and beards.

Below us a small stream flowed slowly through the temple grounds, with steps descending from the temple down to the stream. Standing on the bank of the stream, I noticed a cremation ceremony below, with a man tending the embers of a fire. I said prayers for the deceased as well as his family. I wanted to watch without being a voyeur—perhaps I could be classified as an interested spectating mourner. This was the first Buddhist funeral site I had ever seen. The man tending the small flames used a broom-like rake to tamp the fire. I could see no evidence of a body or burial clothes among the smoking pile of ash, wood, and fire. I wondered about the person who died. I offered prayers for the family, which probably included the man tending the fire. "May the deceased see his God face to face," I prayed, respecting the person's faith belief. Our guide explained about the temple and I tried to listen while watching the man tending the pyre.

Months later in my ministerial life I would be asked to conduct a funeral for a Hindu woman in connection with my ministry at St. Vincent Jennings Hospital. Nepal has a large Hindu population. The woman, a patient at the hospital, died there. The patient's husband asked me to conduct her service at a local funeral home. There was no pyre or burning. Before the funeral, I did research and incorporated some Hindu prayers into the ceremony. Immediately, the family and friends picked up on the words I spoke and repeated them in a chant. Afterward, the widower said he was most grateful to me for the service, because no Hindu ministerial person was available to him and his family. He said he appreciated the way I was present for him at the hospital and that was why he chose me. It didn't seem to matter to this Hindu widower that I was a Catholic Christian.

As I watched the solitary man tending the fire in Kathmandu, I hoped he had someone to companion him—Buddhist, Hindu, or otherwise, and that he had a non-judgmental listener to walk with him. He seemed quite by himself. I hoped it didn't matter that a Catholic Christian was present and praying for him.

Our guide said it was time to move on, so I nodded my head in blessing to this Hindu man. "Prayers for: grace, mercy, peace, faith for you and the family;" This is a prayer I still pray daily for many families who have lost loved ones.

When we entered and left this second holy site, hawkers were everywhere selling all manner of goods. And the ones we saw on this day were especially aggressive. So my Sunday worship (plus yesterday's two-fer) was happily and sadly marked in an inter-faith manner, tinged with an entrepreneurship born of making a living. Again, I recalled my hope for diversity, a wish already granted, and remembered the words of one of my teachers: "There's more that unites us than separates us. But we tend to concentrate on what separates us rather than what unites us."

I was grateful to have a view permitting me to me see the unity of all. I added to my original prayer, "Please enlarge this answer to my prayer as big as you wish, won't you God of all, God of many names."

After going to "church," I had a date at the airport where I hoped another prayer would be favorably considered. And praise the Lord and rock and roll, my bags had arrived without incident. Customs waved me through with nary a peek at anything and I still had time that afternoon to organize my gear. I thanked God I was able to let it go and enjoy my visit without being troubled by unnecessary angst. I also thanked Him for the spiritual growth.

I had dinner with several crew members and went off to bed early. For me, the next day would feel like Christmas morning—a time to open the gifts. We would depart the Shangri-la hotel for the airport, board a propeller plane, and take a 30 minute flight to Lukla. My much anticipated trek to Mount Everest would officially begin.

Monday, 30 April, 2007

After a good night of little boy sleep, I awakened at 4:30 a.m. feeling vibrantly alive. This was the day I had trained for during the last six months. I ate a hearty breakfast and by 6:45 a.m., nine trekkers, all our luggage, and four guides crowded into vehicles and motored to the Kathmandu Airport.

Our vehicles stopped away from the commercial passenger side, at a gate set aside for mountain expeditions. The weather had socked in Lukla, our destination, so we waited. I told myself, "I've waited on this since September, so a few more minutes or hours (but I hope not days) won't matter." Even though I felt eager and expectant, even child-like with giddiness and anticipation, I was a relaxed waiter, prayerful with my extra time. And, I also squeezed in a nap. This was the biggest adventure in my life, and even though I had a reservoir filled with eagerness, I stayed content and calm. I amused myself by wondering which mountaineering giants had waited in the chairs we occupied.

Would Hillary have waited in these very chairs back when I was five years old in 1953? Probably not. The room looked too new for that and I remembered back then that Lukla was reached by foot from Kathmandu.) But since the inaugural summit by Hillary and Tenzing, only a few hundred climbers have reached the top. Many of them flew to Lukla where the airport now bears the names of its first summiteers.

After a 3.5 hour wait and a couple of naps and many prayers, we received a boarding call. First we bussed from the gate to the plane, then boarded the plane, which contained a few rows of snug, two-by-two seats. I reminded myself the airplane engines would be the last engine noise we heard for a while. Soon those engines started and we flew into a cloudy Himalayan sky. Dorzee and our nine trekkers flew together; the rest of the guides and porters would meet us at Lukla.

Oh, my God. The Himalayan range stretched out before us, snow-capped mountains all around. Lesser and lower peaks had green vegetation from their oxygenated surroundings. After a little over 20 minutes we prepared for landing. The word was passed from the pilot to the first row, second row, and so on.

Yeti was the airline's name. Hmmm. Yeti is the folk tale of huge creatures that roam these mountains, said to be part human, and also called the abominable snowman. It's reported he (or she?) leaves deep, oversize tracks in the Himalayan snow. Sightings have been recorded. Scientists and critics contend Yeti is a classic hoax borne of imagination—perhaps the product of too little sleep and too much alcohol. Yet, Yeti's hairy face is painted on the airliners that bear his name. So he has a face, a name, and a legend. Hmm. I wonder if Yeti is related to Bigfoot, or if he is Bigfoot on an expedition out of North America to Asia.

Lukla, our landing point (I hope and pray), is ranked as the most dangerous airport in the world for landings and takeoffs. Did I say in the entire world? This airport has one of the highest elevations for an airport in the world, featuring an incredibly short runway with a significant uphill grade for planes on approach. The runway is narrow and sharp, with a 90 degree right-hand turn a few meters before a mountainside awaits the unprepared pilot. This uphill danger also means a significant downhill grade for aircraft takeoffs that jump off in a rush, like a diver springing from the end of a board. The deep ravine of thousands of meters has led to tragedies for many planes and passengers.

The weather at the Lukla airport can go bad in a hurry. And for an airport of such small size it handles a high volume of fixed wing aircraft and helicopters, each of them fully loaded with climbers and expedition gear. Did I say: The pilot has to stand on the brakes immediately after landing so the plane doesn't roll into the mountainside that marks the end of the runway. All a good reason to pray for safety: "Dear God..."

The ten of us and our gear were shoehorned into this small plane especially designed for landing sites like Lukla with short take-offs and landings. We were almost sitting on top of one another as we readied to land. This plane had the engines mounted above the wings for maneuverability. We landed with a jolt on touchdown, and as the pilot braked to a stop we all pitched forward. Some of us then were sitting on top of one another.

All in a morning's work for Yeti Airlines. For this Yeti plane and pilot, I said, "Thank you, I am safe." I didn't care to learn the morbidity and mortality statistics for landings and take-offs at Lukla. Knowing its reputation was enough.

In this same area, a plane crash killed the wife and young daughter of Sir Edmund Hillary, the first man to summit Everest with Tenzing. The airport at Lukla now bears their names. As a pastoral care hospital chaplain who worked a great deal with parents who lost children, I wondered about the spiritual support Sir Edmund and his family received after this tragic loss. The humanitarian that he was leads me to believe he and his family received wonderful support. He would've been surrounded by other humanitarians, I think. Sir Edmund showed generosity and love to the Sherpa people by building schools, medical clinics, and hospitals, prompting me to think he found peace from his work that surpassed all understanding, as the Gospel writer suggests. Was his example not worthy of a Nobel Peace Prize, I wonder?

The weather brightened as we deplaned. We claimed our bags and hiked a little ways to a tea house for, well, tea, and some lunch. It was a cool spring day in Lukla with the sun playing peek-a-boo and temps in the 50s maybe 60s. I was a little hungry, but hunger wasn't the most important thing on my mind. The scenery captivated me—the Himalayan mountains surrounding us. I had visited the mountains of Colorado and the Andes in Chile to ski, but here there are no ski lifts. Where ever you go from Lukla, you go by foot because there also are no cars, four wheelers, or snowmobiles. You see—there are no roads. And already I could see poverty. Yet I also saw joy on the faces of these native Nepalese hill people. I didn't see this so much in Kathmandu. Here, I would see it every day as we trekked thru small and larger villages. The occupants seemed happy, especially the children, though some of their houses had dirt floors.

And I too felt joyful, because as soon as we finished lunch, we would begin our trek.

The sun came out to greet us as we stepped off on a two week plus trek to Mount Everest Base Camp. The sun stayed with us much of the day, providing enough warmth that I felt comfortable in shorts, a fleece pullover atop a T-shirt, a ball cap, and trek boots. I carried a back pack and what the Aussie "kids" taught me to call sunnys; Aussie-speak for sunglasses.

Our first order of business on the mountain had little to do with trekking and more to do with politics. At the time of our trek, the Department of State of the United States federal government had issued an alert to Americans travelling to Nepal. This was not a travel ban, although such a ban was next on the list in State's warning system. It was a stern warning. The last few years and this year had seen beatings and even killings, in the Everest area, including tourists. This was blamed in part on Chinese muscle exerting influence and force within the ruling regime of Nepal. The aggressors were thugs and robbers who could, and did, make life hard for mountaineers, who were essentially tourists. The elite athletes going to the top or trekkers like us with a different mountain vision, were a mix of internationals who presumably carried cash. People on holiday, no matter what their vision, had been robbed, beaten, and even killed. Thus, State's warning. The stupidity was that mountaineers gave the Nepali economy a huge infusion of cash. The beatings and killings threatened this.

We made a short stop at a post set up on the side of the trail where a bed sheet hung with writing on it in red paint. I didn't know what it said. Dorzee, by his instruction to us, did the talking to the people at the post, which numbered several men. I never saw any money exchange hands, and I never asked. I hung to the back of our group during this stop. I knew about the "Maoists" as these people were called. Whatever happened, it happened quietly. There were no outbursts or overt action. Dorzee was an experienced guide, we'd been told. I figured this wasn't his first rodeo and the best course of action was to stay out of the way and let him do the talking as he wanted. We were there only a few minutes. And without incident, we were back on our way—downhill. Downhill, you ask?

You might think mountain climbing, especially at Everest, is all about going uphill. But upon leaving Lukla the first thing we did was descend more than 500 feet. An unusual way to get my legs stretched out, I thought. I knew there were downhill sections—I just hadn't expected one in the beginning. And what goes down must climb up. We regained the 500 foot descent and still kept going up. This was more of what I expected, although downhill sounded easier. In fact, hiking downhill is often difficult for me because it requires a different set of muscles and sometimes weakens my knees and causes my shins to ache.

Day one at Everest was fully under way. Not only did we go uphill after our downhill start, there were—gulp—two suspension bridges to cross. These flimsy bridges seemed alive as they swayed right and left. That was a challenge for me, but good preparation for the bridges ahead, especially as we neared Namche Bazaar.

These bridges are made of thick cables suspended from pilings on either side of a gorge or river. Above, and parallel to these big cables, runs a second set of lighter weight cables. Vertical cables connect the two sets. The bridge floor is constructed laterally across the strong bottom set of cables. The floor might be fabricated steel, but more often was made of sawed wooden planks. Sometimes the planks were missing. Gulp again.

The bridges move as you walk across them, typically swaying sideways. They also bounce up and down when heavier people or yak transport animals enter the bridge at the same time, causing a ripple effect like a wave pulsing and washing ashore. While wind can and does move them, the motion of people or yaks usually causes the bridge's motion—and that is only one of the challenges involved in crossing.

Another issue, a big one for me, was their height above the river and the gorge below. Some of these bridge crossings literally took my breath away.

Passing on the bridge was another challenge, because each passer-by has to edge to the side. While wearing a backpack, turning this way or that did no good and the bridges are less than two people wide, which made for delicate maneuvering.

I soon discovered one does not enter a bridge if yaks are coming in the other direction. Yaks or Dzomo (yaks cross-bred with cattle) equal the weight of a sub-compact car and sport horns that can each stretch two feet long. They are the original "wide body."

Mischief also can create a challenge. This day it was children well behind us having fun by jumping up and down like the bridge was a trampoline. This sent a surge through the bridge floor. The first time I felt this ripple effect, I thought I'd be launched into space. I didn't know if we were having an earthquake until I heard Deckland and Ingrid laughing. *Not funny,* I told myself. "Oh, geez!" I whispered.

The second bridge crossing was worse than the first, and this had nothing to do with kids. This time the floor was made of wood planks, with some of the planks missing in action. "Oh, geez!" magnified. I prayed, prayed, and prayed some more, because on this bridge the cables were too low for a proper handhold. Behind me, Tom uttered supportive words that kept me going.

The trail to Everest connected tidy little villages, some containing dry mortar stone buildings trimmed in wood. A few had window glass, but many windows contained no screen or glass, just rough cut openings. Several buildings had brightly painted solid accent colors of orange, purple, yellow, or red. The building shapes blended with each other and their design seemed to merge with the mountains, while their colors contrasted with nature. This made for a delightful mix. Colorful Buddhist prayer flags fluttered in the villages and from high points on the hilltops.

In a few areas the trek path seemed to have been laid out with stones fitted together. Usually the trail was dirt about two, maybe three-people-wide in most spots. Walls occasionally lined the trail, but generally not. Looking over the side of the trail caused a reality check. In some places the drop off was a couple hundred feet. Up here, of course, we had no 911 service.

The scenery included mountains, hillsides, ravines, and rivers. We down climbed and for a while were 30 or so feet above the water level of the Dudh Kosi River. Pronounced "Dude Coat-see," the name translated to "Milk River" because of its mostly white color and creamy looking texture. The color resulted from the glacial melt of the Everest area region of the Himalayan range that fed the river. I amended its proper name translation to "Milk Shake River." The water always seemed to be rocking and rolling, shaking and twisting as it tumbled through a riverbed riveted with boulders as large as 2.5 ton trucks. These huge rocks were strewn throughout the river bed as if loosed from the hand of a giant playing a game of marbles. This geologic hubris of marbles made the swollen river bounce, or "shake," all the more.

We passed working yaks, grazing ponies, rambunctious baby goats, and pecking chickens. We saw orchids and tiny flowers the size of fingernails. The minute size, the animated life and the colors were in stark contrast to the sheer mass of the mountains, their charcoal color; the solid non-movement of sentinels standing at parade rest in jagged formation. We heard birdsong and the rushing of the swollen river tumbling over the huge rocks. We felt a refreshing breeze. I tasted the cold water I carried.

We trekked for three and a half hours on the first day—a good warm-up. Finally we reached our destination for the evening; a teahouse at a little village called Phakding at 7,956 feet elevation.

For perspective, we were higher than Denver with its elevation of 5,280 feet (a mile high). And we were still 10,000 feet below Everest Base Camp. I had a little tightness, a muscle pain, in my left shoulder blade from the backpack, but otherwise I felt fine.

Our tea house, or lodge, had a kind of beer garden we used appropriately, with a number of us ordering the "Everest" brand beer, which had a great flavor. A near full moon was rising, but I didn't linger to watch it. Most of us went off to bed by 8 p.m. I had a compact little room with twin beds—one for me and the other for my luggage. As everyone had a roommate except me, I didn't share sleeping quarters on the trek. This was mostly okay, although loneliness did plague me. That night I slept for nine hours and only needed to find the loo once. Thankfully, this was not a primitive loo. We actually had a flushable toilet mounted on a concrete floor, which would soon become a rarity.

Tuesday, 1 May, 2007

Nine hours of sound sleep, and I felt absolutely great in the morning, especially when I stepped outside my room and saw the white snow-capped Himalayan peaks atop wide grayish mountains everywhere I looked—a dazzling sight with blue skies and a bright yellow-white sun for accent color. The air was brisk, with no wind.

That day's morning trek took us past several waterfalls, tiny, small, big, and bigger—like *Goldilocks and the Three Bears* gone aquatic. Morning sunlight turned the papa bear waterfall into a giant prism, filtering the light with visual amplification giving it vivid color and beauty. The theologian chapel designer in me thought, *What a beautiful natural stained glass window!*

We hiked for three hours from Phakding to Moonjo, during which our elevation gain was a mere 600 feet. However, following lunch we had a vigorous acclimatizing walk, going upward 1,000-

plus feet. As we walked upward I realized we are being evaluated by Dorzee, who studied each of us closely to see how we handled this mini climb. We rested at a "saddle," or level spot, to hydrate, visit, and shoot pics. This acclimatizing hike allowed us to "climb high and sleep low," a proven method for the human body to adjust to thinning air without risking illness that can be serious, even deadly.

I made two unwelcome discoveries during our morning walk: Some of us talked more than others, and the talkers seemed to use a loud decibel level. The volume made me wonder if some of my fellow hikers were hearing impaired, although I noticed no hearing aid devices. Often the talk was about mundane things like television shows, movies, and favorite actors and actresses. Not having had a television in my home for eight years and not being a movie-goer, I found this tedious.

I didn't want to be judgmental, nor did I want to have my trek spoiled by trashy language, so I went proactive with my non-listening skills—tuning out voices as one would ignore elevator music. When this didn't fully work, I changed my pace to get ahead of, or behind, the chatter. I did this because I wanted peace in my life amid this majestic, pristine nature.

I took responsibility for that need without imposing my own desires on others. I wanted silence to hear the birdsong, the singing of the waterfalls we passed, and of the Milk River as it hurtled through the canyon below us, or alongside us. I didn't want to hear about cinema or crude plots and how characters cavorted on screen, and off.

I loved it when Silah, our guide, was ahead of me and I could hear his soft signing, his whistle. As I discovered others had a need to talk loudly about things from home, I also discovered how I could find silence. And when I wished to be engaged in conversation, I could seek that option also. I'd simply catch up with people and join the conversation, or start one.

After lunch, our 1,000+ foot acclimatizing ascent, and then a descent, we took the afternoon off. I had watched Dorzee watching us and he and I exchanged glances. I knew he understood I was aware of what he was doing. Neither of us said anything. I didn't hear anyone mention this, and I didn't either. Maybe they noticed; maybe not.

My afternoon's walk lacked the conversational jolts I'd overheard in the morning. Perhaps going steeply uphill required too much breath for talking. Whatever the reason, I found the going lent itself to what I was calling "meditation in motion." I found a rhythmic pace that allowed me to pray, recite Bible verses, and to feel awed by the beauty of the natural order about us. We moved steadily uphill. Now this was exercise made special, perhaps even sacred, by my internal meditation and the environment of nature provided by God.

Our daytime weather was ideal, although rain fell during the night, so there was some mud about. I watched my footing. My broken-in Scarpa boots, bought in January and trekked in almost every day since, felt great. So far our mountain mornings and evenings were comfortable for my trek clothes. Overnight the thermometer dropped to the 30s and 40s. We had sun much of the day, but again walking felt comfortable. We traveled under the shade of trees during many areas on the trail. I was in bed by about 8 p.m. again, and this time I tucked into my sleeping bag under a full moon, fully enjoying the peace and solitude.

When I drive to St. Vincent Jennings in North Vernon from my home in Columbus, about 25 miles, there are days when I keep the radio turned off, especially during the religious season of Lent. The quiet in my car adds to the peacefulness I feel and lets me further appreciate the beauty of the countryside along this two lane road. The solitude promotes my prayer life. In Paul's letter to the

Philippians in chapter 4 of the New Testament, the Apostle Paul writes:

"Do not be anxious about anything, but in every situation, by prayer and petition, with thanksgiving, present your requests to God. And the peace of God which surpasses all understanding will guard your hearts and your minds in Christ Jesus."

Amen to that, Brother Paul!

9:01 AM

I wondered how the Tibetan Buddhists monks of this area wrote about nature and the peace and beauty it provides. I did know their name for Everest is: "Chomolungma," translated as "Mother Goddess of Earth." To so name a mountain, the tallest on Earth, caused me to believe these holy monks celebrated nature as a part of their beliefs and worship.

However, something I ate was not promoting peace in my GI tract. Awakening from sleep, in the dark, I make an emergency dash to the loo which I scouted out that afternoon on a non-emergency stop. Oh geez—a rookie mistake and stupid: I forgot to carry my "torch" –the flashlight. I hoped I wouldn't step in something. My long term memory of the loo's footprint was fortunately better than my short-term memory about the flashlight. Ah, humility. I tried not to touch anything around me as I groped in the dark. Well, this movement worked out okay in the end—cough. Peace again. It occurred to me that Jesus, as a man, might have had similar GI tract issues. And in this region, the Buddhas as well.

Wednesday, 2 May, 2007

The full moon beamed bright outside my window overnight. Reflecting on this, my journal notes show Scripture verses came to mind. I wrote:

"You God made the heavens and the earth and all that is in them. You count the stars and you call them all by name ... including the greater light (the sun that governs the day) and this lessor light (the moon before me which governs the night). Your mighty hand and your mighty arm made these (Himalayan) mountains all around me. You instruct the waters (the Milk River) to its boundaries (and churning!). Thanks Creator God."

This would be a day with tall—make that high—orders before us. We would ascend 1,500 feet to Namche Bazaar, a kind of "capital" on the trail to Everest. A trading center for generations, what we might call a Saturday Farmer's Market at home is a mobile market of commerce with families and merchants from Nepal and Tibet travelling from afar to trade and sell vegetable produce, woolen goods, salt products, hand crafts, and T-shirts. This outdoor bazaar lasts for a single day.

En route to Namche we crossed three suspension bridges. The most difficult crossing came last—a formidable passage with a high, long, and dipping bridge. In its locale, it looked almost unbelievable. What a big gulp I took as I eyed it to snap a picture. The span stretched about 100 feet above the churning Milk Shake River, upon whose banks we stood. And it was the longest bridge we would cross going to and from Base Camp. I felt my hands go sweaty just viewing it from afar. My buds Deckland and Ingrid, "the kids," and I took pictures of each other from our rest-break vantage point with the bridge for background. The river was so loud we could scarcely hear the words we yelled and repeated to each other.

After our photo shoot, we shouldered our packs and made a steep climb from the riverbed, up a hundred feet and more, to where the bridge crossed the river. On reaching the portal of the bridge and looking across and down, two words crossed my lips (excuse my French): "Holy shit!" Other than that crude expression, I was speechless.

The churning Milk River was in full tumult, foaming and crashing against blocks of boulders the size of quarry blocks from my home of Bedford, Indiana. The glacial melt had the river running high, although the glaciers were still many trek days away, upstream at the Khumbu Icefall.

The Icefall, a deadly frozen river of unbalanced ice blocks and seracs was precariously situated above Everest Base Camp, our destination. Avalanches in the Icefall, tumbling seracs and blocks bigger than big homes, have killed many aspiring climbers, and their faithful Sherpa guides and porters. Now speechless, I gaped at the swollen and noisy river crashing through the gorge maybe one hundred feet down below. I took my first step onto the bridge and aimed my mind elsewhere.

Striking for a positive note, I thought: "I am so blessed to be able to experience this. Pinch me. Is this real?"

"Slow down, partner," the analytical side of my brain said to my theological and appreciative side. "This high and long and maybe rowdy bridge ahead of you promises most challenging next steps. Save your gratitude. Suspend thought. Express it later. The time now is for focus—big time."

"Roger," I responded aloud.

Anxiety grew within me. I had to cross this bridge. No choice. Really, I was speechless. Imagine a swaying bridge constructed of cables 100 feet high, suspended from one shore to the other above a river gorge filled with boulders scattered like litter in the water, waves splashing all about them. The bridge looked a quarter-mile long, maybe longer.

A mix of fear and caution took hold of me. And focus.

I had taken only a few steps onto the bridge when the first person going the opposite direction neared me. Of course people were going both ways, I reminded myself. "Mind your steps, posture, and hand holds." Thankfully, no yaks were coming my way. My naivete said, "There's no such thing as span-sharing." More thanks—I saw the bridge was festooned with colorful Tibetan Buddhist prayer flags, and I needed all the prayers I could get.

Yes, I was apprehensive. By now we'd crossed five or six bridges and I felt more confident putting one foot in front of the other. Not looking down helped a lot, although I wanted to master looking down so I could further appreciate the view. I held on tight to the side cables and said a prayer. I watched my steps while trying not to look below the bridge deck. I heard the water crashing below. I was delicately careful when people passed going the other way, trying not to bump them or get bumped.

Who knows how long the crossing took? Forever, it seemed. I began to relax a little as the other side of the bridge was maybe 50 yards away. Below, I saw we were across the river and land was starting to come back up to meet us. Terra firma land was only a few feet below me as we neared where the heavy bridge cables were securely anchored into the mountainside.

As we reached the end of crossing over the bridge, having cleared the river gorge, I showed off a little with a 360 degree ballerina turn, first left and then right. I even did a little dance. Silly showing off, I told myself, but it helped me build confidence. I didn't care who was behind me watching. I did the sillies for my own self as a kind of graduation stroll to pick up a diploma as "Pomp and Circumstance" played in the background. So much better for my self-esteem than feeling panic and peril. Plus, I knew we'd be crossing the same bridge again on our way back.

Following my pirouettes we reached the end of the bridge, but I had little time to celebrate. Immediately we had another task—a 30 minute uphill climb that went almost straight up, laid out in a combination of steps and trail—a trail dotted with gnarled tree roots that actually helped provide footing. One word described both steps and trail: Steep, with a capital S. The climb was grueling.

Still, I noticed something. And what I had observed stuck with me. People heading past me toward the bridge we'd crossed were going downhill. Down and down—downhill. I seem to remember actually coming to a stop to observe this. In about two weeks' time that would be me going downhill; returning home. God willing, I would be returning from Everest Base Camp, still healthy and strong. I would have come back through Namche Bazaar and I expected in some ways to be different person.

For now, the grind of the climb to Namche continued. Up, up, and up some more. The thrill of the bridge crossing was erased by the tedious slog. Nonetheless, the accomplishment of the bridge challenge gave me propulsion for this climb.

To enter Namche, we walked through a colorfully painted wooden pedestrian gate of welcome to this storied little village. Not far away was a shallow open trench sewer, diminishing the welcome gate a bit. Namche sits on a steep hillside and the locals have ingeniously terraced the hill-land to accommodate houses and vegetable gardens. There is a large mercantile area of maybe a hundred retail shops, restaurants, bars, banks, internet service providers, grocers, and I saw one butcher shop.

As we walked through the village, I paused for a moment before the butcher shop's "window," which was an un-glassed opening in the wall. I observed trade occurring through the open door and windows, hearing and seeing the whack of the butcher's cleaver. Tea houses and hotels nestled here and there within the maze of shops. One of those hotels was ours, conveniently near what seemed to be the crossroads of local commerce. Our front door opened onto the stone sidewalk that doubled as the pathway to Everest.

At lunch I consumed carbs with an appetite worthy of a yak, the strong four-legged transport creature the size of a bull with the strength of an elephant. An afternoon rain soon prompted an afternoon nap. My narrow room had twin beds with clean white sheets—what luxury. My other overnight teahouse lodgings had couches or beds, but my sleeping bag went atop their tattered blankets. These beds even have bed pillows, instead of throw pillows you might see on a couch. I took a great power nap until the rain stopped, and then out the door I went. It was time for power shopping.

I did my part to bolster the Namche economy in a small way. I bought T-shirts, woolen goods, a yak bell (which to this day hangs on the inside of my kitchen door where I hung it on my return), bracelets, slippers, pendants, things for daughters-in-law, sons, and friends. Oops, rainfall resumed. So I ducked out of the rain and bought a beer. The rain stopped and shopping resumed. I finished the shopping spree buying gifts for myself. I spotted some of the crew and we all took turns getting group photo shots. "Be careful, mind the yak dung" I warned as one of our photographers backed up without looking—and we all laughed as he barely avoided a misstep into a pile of it. Yaks walk these streets carrying their loads just as the trekkers and climbers do. Who cleans up their mess? Good question, I don't know that anyone does.

The sidewalk stone pathway of the trail to Everest winds through Namche, connecting one end of town to the other. This trail is the route anyone heading to Everest will follow. Shopkeepers, customers, Buddhist monks in their purple and yellow robes, children, expeditions big and small, individual trekkers, heck even Sir Ed Hillary and Tenzing Norgay walked through Namche also. The elite men and elite women mountaineers come this way, including the iconic English who were knighted. We commoners walked here also. And so, I stepped my feet among boot prints in the land of giants—men women, and mountains. How humbling for an almost senior citizen Hoosier. And so also the load-bearing yaks tread through here. And when they "gotta go," they do, wherever they might be, including where we shot "snaps" as some of the Aussies referred to recording our historic moment.

Maybe it was what I saw before issuing my warning, the power of suggestion on seeing the yak crap. Maybe it was just time. Maybe it was something else. But in an instant after our snap was shot I knew I needed a bathroom—and I needed it immediately.

I made it just in time to our hotel, the second floor, and the "common," meaning shared by the lodging community, bathroom. Uh oh—cramps and diarrhea. Not good! How'd this happen? Diarrhea had to be something I ate. Or drank. Uh oh. I remembered I didn't wipe the top of the beer can to clean it, nor did I pour the beverage into a clean glass after wiping the can. What did my guide book say about beverages? Such stupidity. Arrgh. I did myself in.

I migrated not far from the restroom to the common area that doubled as the dining room. Members of my group showed concern and commiserate with my compromising dis-ease. Oops, no time to talk now. I returned to the bathroom in a hurry. Again. From that episode a nap sounded like a good idea. Trina of our group found Dorzee and sent him to my room. He asked questions about how I was feeling. In the process he did something to me and for me—something I did for patients at St. Vincent Jennings Hospital. The sirdar, expedition leader went beyond his expected role and provided me with pastoral care.

As I lay on my clean white sheets, Dorzee touched my abdomen with his left hand and asked, "Is there where it hurts?"

"Yes," I responded as he put he put his hand exactly on my GI tenderness. Keeping his hand lightly on my abdomen, he asked me questions about my diet, about the beer, some medical stuff, and then he asked about the trek. Was I enjoying myself? What did I think about the things I was seeing? All the while he lightly kept his hand on my abdomen.

We visited for 10, perhaps 15, minutes and his hand never left my gut, the pressure always the same. He had a pleasant countenance throughout and smiled periodically.

Then he asked, "Do you feel better?"

I did, both emotionally and physically, and I said so. He smiled. He'd been sitting on my bed, and as he rose, for the first time since he placed his hand on my area of discomfort, he removed it. Hmmm, it definitely felt better.

"What just happened," I asked myself? I received comfort from someone who visited the sick—me.

I couldn't nap then, and it wasn't just the "niggles" as the Aussies nicknamed my malady. I felt achy and fever-y, very uncomfortable. I returned to the common area where members of our group had gathered, and there was sincere inquiry about my health. My young friend Deckland counseled, "Sleep it off."

Slightly offended, I said "I didn't choose this like a drunken rout and hangover." Deckland, now also offended, responded, "In Australia this kind of 'sleep it off' means sleep 'til you're well.'"

"Oh, I see. Thank you," I said, and equilibrium between us was restored.

Trina, who lost her husband to cancer after 20 years of marrige offered to keep an eye on me. I thanked her, but passed on the offer. She tucked me in just the same, and said she would check in on me. "It's not good to be sick and by yourself." I remember one of her two visits to check on me.

That morning, as we trekked and climbed up to Namche I felt the dynamic within the group seemed good. My experience with sickness confirmed it and I notched the grade higher. Later, on returning through Namche to go down that big hill out of town to the bridge, I would have different feelings about this. For the moment though, I was at peace.

I rested. I awakened and made two bathroom pit stops during the night. My symptoms were subsiding. I was moving from disease toward ease again. Beautiful moonlight streamed through a tall window, flooding into my room. As Dorzee's hand on my intestines provided comfort, the moonlight infused my spirit.

Thursday, 3 May, 2007

How long did I sleep? About ten hours, except for my GI ups and downs. Not little boy sleep quality that's for sure. But I did feel better, with only a bit of lurking residual crampy stuff, but not the awfulness of yesterday. I said prayers of gratitude, plus petitions for" better still, if you please, God."

Trina asked, "How are you?" I provide her an update. Ron asked too. And Ingrid. And I gave them my update.

Trina, however, asked an additional question: "You going today?" She pointedly got to the heart of the matter.

"Planning on it," I said keeping my words simple and expectant. Hope is always so important to me.

Trina's question of "Going today" translated to another acclimatizing hike, and that meant going upward. We were at 10,300 and would go to 12,700 feet that day. My personal record for elevation was 14,500 down in Chile when I was skiing, and that was gained with helicopter assist. Today would be a 2,300+ elevation gain. And I wondered how my GI tract would respond. "Please, God—healing!"

In addition to prayers, I drank and drank water and kept my food intake simple. Apparently that's what I needed to do. Between the Ps, practicality and prayer, I felt good to go. All the hydration helped flush me clean. Prayers kept me connected spiritually, "And thank you," I added.

We were gone for a few hours. As we climbed above a forest onto a small saddle of level ground, suddenly we saw the top of Everest in clear view. It showed up silently, like a sunrise or sunset when you aren't paying attention, with no clap of thunder or drumroll. But there it was, with a mantle of white on Everest's shoulders. The jet stream must have had the day off because the signature plume that consists of ice, snow, and rock was not blowing from its peak like a pennant in the wind.

"Pinch me," I said aloud, mostly to myself. I wanted my voice to sear the message on my psyche. What I saw before me in real life surpassed all pictures and words about Everest. The mountain itself stood proud and tall before me, probably 15 linear miles away, yet with lots of up and down in between—and mostly up. But the tallest thing on the planet appears closer than it is. Everest's sheer mass was breath-taking. With feet in both Nepal and Tibet it was bigger than some states.

Before we drew closer to Everest, Dorzee had us rest at the saddle view. It was difficult to take my eyes off the prize. Yet, as I found a rock to sit on, I saw nature celebrating the arrival of spring at the other end of Earth's size spectrum. Tiny purple and yellow crocus the size of coinage dotted the landscape near my dusty boots. I witnessed a study in contrasts of color, size, and beauty with Chomolungma, Everest's Tibetan name. Instead of uplifted rock crowned by ice 5.5 miles or 29,035 feet high, I saw alpine flowers poke an inch or two above the ground. Creation had demonstrated its versatility, providing me with bass and treble: Huge and small, gray-black-white, and muted colors. I touched the small, colorful petals with one finger. Perhaps mountains and flowers, biggest and tiny, had co-existed here here since time began, ageless, diverse, dormant, and alive. The flowers returned every spring, and Everest is said to rise higher by about half an inch every year from tectonic plates miles below the earth sliding from India under Asia, edging Everest higher and higher with microscopic small growth spurts.

After the break we continued climbing. Well above Namche, we crossed an airfield—a strip of sod used primarily by visitors to the nearby Everest View Hotel. The hotel has an amazing view of Everest and the panorama of peaks about it—Nuptse, 25,000, Lhotse, 27,000, Ama Dablam, 22,000 in round numbers. The panoramic peaks create a stunning view.

Oops! I spoke too soon. Clouds moved in and obscured our view as we got situated for group pics. The background was an absolute once-in-a-lifetime keeper Kodak moment. I got out in front and orchestrated positions for everyone so we were all in the picture, along with Everest. The group seemed to appreciate the leadership to get a best picture. Snaps shot, we had a round of tea. The wind picked up and I slipped a parka on and tied a bandanna around my face as dust particles were blowing about.

Going back downhill it was "Zoom, Zoom!" as Rajhud one of the younger guides liked to say to prod us into action after a break. I noticed he picked up from me the words "Time to rock and roll," which I said to anyone who was listening whenever we stepped off. Rajud had black, shiny Elvis-like hair. He echoed me "Time to rock and roll" with a big smile. Going downhill seemed effortless and one guy, Mike, even broke into a run.

Back at Namche, some of us shopped some more. I think I overstepped cultural commerce understanding when in a bargaining process I tried to take a shopkeeper lower than she wished to go. She insisted on her higher price, so I declined and walked away. I hope I didn't break mercantile decorum. She seemed agitated. Maybe it was just a bad day at her shop.

The next day, a rest day on our own, a few of us took an uphill hike to a kind of nature museum located next to a military compound surrounded by razor wire. What a contrast—the peace of nature and the military's might next door. On the way back down to Namche, I saw a lodge I'd noticed on the way up. Remembering its location and name, I believed it was the one owned by the parents of the man who befriended me on the plane, Tenzing of Denver. I left my group, went into the lodge, asked for the owner, and introduced myself to he and his wife. They were in fact Tenzing's parents, who spoke some English and seemed so pleased to make my acquaintance. They invited me to tea, and we visited for a couple of cups before I made my farewell. They were kind, so appreciative of my stopping to say hello. Their lodge was beautiful in a simple way; immaculately clean and fairly new. Located on a knoll above Namche itself, it was unlike the buildings grouped together within the kind of terraced teacup that Namche is. Their lodge was off by itself, as if claustrophobia would be a problem.

That night I was in bed by eight p.m., a welcome pattern for me. And per the pattern, I slept like a little boy. Trekking and elevation seemed to agree with my sleep habits, once the GI problem left my system.

Friday, 4 May, 2007

On this day, my appreciation of nature and worship of its Maker shifted to manmade sacred places. Our destination was Tengboche Monastery, a revered holy place for worship and study by monks of the Tibetan Buddhist faith. A day's journey from Namche Bazaar, the monastery's monks were seen every day in Namche, shopping, visiting the faithful, perhaps just getting away from the monastery's holy grind for the day, and buying supplies. Seeing the monks at Namche was a prelude to our trek to the monastery and staying the night on its holy grounds.

I personally know the significance a monastery may represent to one's faith. Such a monastery is central to my journey. Between Louisville, Kentucky, and Evansville, Indiana, about two hours from my home, nestled in the rolling terrain of southern Indiana is St. Meinrad Archabbey and its School of Theology. St. Meinrad is an internationally recognized teaching center for Benedictine priestly formation, as well as lay graduate study. It also has a retreat center. I received my graduate degree there, but even before that I was on its grounds as a retreatant.

My seminary at St. Meinrad was founded and run by Benedictine monks more than 150 years ago. The first monks migrated there from Switzerland to support first generation European Catholics who populated the southern Indiana area as farmers. I graduated in 2006, the year I heard the "voice" calling me to Everest. My reading hours before the voice were filled with theology texts, as I studied for seminary classes.

On graduating and signing on for this trek, I soon found mountaineering literature a welcome substitute for theology texts. Within the body of work on mountaineering, few books examined the spiritual side of mountaineering. After turning all those pages in seminary theology texts for study, this discovery about mountain literature was curious to me, because the mountains in general, and places like Tengboche, seemed so close to God.

I eagerly awaited my visit to this revered Buddhist center. Unlike Kathmandu's urban sacred centers, I did my homework on Tengobche and knew exactly where we were going.

But first we had a significant down-climb before lunch. Along the way we stopped at a stupa, or worship site, built by Tenzing Norgay, who summited Everest in 1953 with Hillary. This stupa honors Tenzing's grandfather. I had read books by Tenzing, by Hillary, and by Tenzing's son Jamling.

At Tengboche, my twins interests of mountain exploring and spirituality were about to intersect. After our down climb to lunch, we made a steady and steep ascent of 2.5 hours that ended at the monastery. This reminded me in the New Testament of the Hebrew people going "up" to the Temple which was a couple of thousand feet higher on a hill in an area called the Temple Mount.

Once again, I had stomach cramps and had to go behind a large rock for privacy and relief. Thankfully this was not serious. Was it a return of my niggles in Namche, or maybe just a cramp from something I ate since that didn't sit quite right? I didn't know, but it quickly passed.

As we neared the summit of our final hill a "steeple" came into view. With each uphill step a little more of the tapered spire showed. Gold colored, it gave off a muted kind of gleaming in the day's sunlight. I recognized that steeple; we were nearing Tengboche.

I instantly remembered a similar occurrence while biking in the hills around my seminary. As I rode through the country roads, cornfields, and rolling terrain around St. Meinrad, I spotted something that resembled a cornstalk projecting above the fields. Gold colored, it stood out from the green corn.

I was puzzled at first, but soon recognized a cross on top and decided this had to be one of the country churches found in southern Indiana. Yet, this steeple kept getting taller as I approached. Soon I saw the church building and realized I'd ridden into the village of Ferdinand, which has its own monastic community of Benedictine women.

The tall steeple of Tengboche slowly revealed itself as we climbed toward it. As we viewed it from below, I also knew the men and women summiting Everest, on a perfectly clear day, could look downward and see the steeple and monastery from near the summit. We climbed to the top of the hill before us, and suddenly the monastery and its grounds came into full view as we reached 12,600 feet.

This elevation was about one vertical mile below our destination of 17,600 at Everest Base Camp. We were now almost 2.5 miles higher than my home in Indiana.

Several extraordinary spiritual blessings awaited me at the storied monastery, which was once nearly destroyed by earthquake, and a second time was damaged by fire. Coincidentally, my seminary at Meinard also had a devastating fire early in its history.

But first came a remarkable surprise. Before making this trip, one of my hopes for Everest Base Camp was to meet people coming down from the summit and hear their stories. I didn't have to wait until Base Camp to talk to one of the Everest climbers. At Tengboche, I overheard Johan, a climber from Sweden, who was heading up to climb Everest, talking to Karl, his base camp manager. They had down climbed from Base Camp to the more oxygenated air in this valley and were over-nighting at the monastery grounds before heading back up to prepare for Johan's ascent. I politely interrupted and asked if we could talk for a moment about what Johan's Everest experience was like.

Karl teased (I think he was teasing) and said he'd have to charge me for the interview. Johan's plan was to summit Everest without oxygen—a difficult feat accomplished by only a few people including my American hero climber Ed Viesturs from Seattle. Johan was climbing all the Seven Summits without oxygen. If he succeeded, he'd belong to an exclusive club. I would later figure out I wished to do this as well, with oxygen of course, preposterous as it sounded. Perhaps hearing Johan personally speak planted this idea in my subconscious. He only had Everest and the Vinson Massif in Antarctica left. I believe I remember hearing him say that training and attitude were the keys. On my return to America I checked the evertesnews.com website—and sure enough, Johan was credited as a successful summiteer.

Karl ended this interview by saying he had to get Johan somewhere. Later I felt so rotten at Base Camp I couldn't have carried on a conversation with anyone, so I especially appreciated my time with Johan. He was the first climber I'd met who successfully tagged the top of Everest. But not the last. The second was a Hoosier who lived 45 minutes away from me, who had friends in Columbus with a business a couple of blocks from me.

This beginning to my time at Tengboche presented a non-spiritual surprise and a good one. Did the divine have another surprise in store for me, perhaps a spiritual one, I wondered? After all this was holy ground.

I anticipated the worship service, so that wasn't a surprise. Yet it was certainly filled with sacred moments.

We arrived in late afternoon as people from all over the grounds began moving toward the monastery building—monks and climbers alike. I had no problem telling the difference: trekkers and climbers were outfitted in trekking clothes, while the monks wore saffron and ticket stub yellow colored robes. All of us streamed into the temple—a large, squat building decorated with prayer banners. Sculpted dragon-like figures of wood guarded the entry portal. I expected an afternoon prayer service awaited us, just like at my seminary St. Meinrad's Abbey Church. Meinrad has an evening time for prayer, and so it was with the Buddhists. Heck they've been doing this longer than Christians. Perhaps Christians learned it from the Buddhists.

Monks occupied the center of the square worship space which opened at one end toward an altar with ornate, beautifully painted wooden carvings, including a giant-sized depiction of Buddha. The space was dim to dark as there were no electrical lights. Windows admitted light here and there, along with butter lamps and candles. We visitors sat beyond the perimeter near the walls. After a processional entry, the monks made prostrations toward the figure of the Buddha, much the way we Catholics bow or genuflect when entering a church.

This was the ceremony many trekkers and climbers attended. Perhaps some came here out of curiosity. Others sought God, I expect. During worship the monks chanted aloud, sometimes accompanied by instruments. They also prayed aloud. The service had a certain rhythm to it, though nothing was in English, so I couldn't tell when they were praying or just speaking. During this worship time I had a feeling of connection with the divine through the monks' sacredness. I knew I was witnessing and participating in a timeless sacred liturgy that had been part of their faith for centuries.

Worship, like music, has a universal language. Did I need to understand the words? It might have held more meaning for me on an intellectual level, but faith comes from the heart and leaves room for mystery. I appreciated what I was allowed to observe and experience. I added my own prayers within my own tradition and my own tongue, and then cobbled my prayers with those offered by the monks believing, as the Old Testament says, they all would lift like incense to heaven. I believe that God, who pre-dates language and the confusion it caused at a tower building, and the harmony it resulted in at Pentecost, will sort the prayers out as they rise to Him in whatever dance, language, sacrifice, action, or form they assume.

For all the awe I felt from the liturgy, I may have committed a gaffe. When I shot a picture and more than one during the liturgy, a Western critic seated nearby thought I committed a blunder. Did I? On entry to the Temple, our trek leadership indicated photography during the liturgy was acceptable. So I shot some pics with a small flash that brought a judge-and-jury stern look from a nearby woman trekker. I don't know what she mouthed, but her frown said it all.

Our leader understood temple photography differently, and he gave permission. Well, if I did something wrong I apologized to Buddha. Wrongly or rightly, I have not deleted those pictures from my computer files. I still look at them and marvel at where I was blessed to witness and worship.

I visited with a monk after the service, first asking his permission in case he had taken a vow of partial silence like the Trappist monks I know at Snowmass, Colorado. I wanted to make sure it was alright to begin a conversation with the Buddhist monk who stood beside me. He said it was fine, and he spoke English.

I told him of the Tibetan Buddhist Center near my home in Bloomington, Indiana, and the Dali Lama having visited there several times. I spoke of being in His Holiness' presence when he conducted an interfaith peace worship service at St. Charles Parish Church in 1999. The monk didn't have a lot to say, or perhaps his English was limited. Rats—I'd hoped for dialogue. I did receive the information I sought about a morning prayer service. I had surmised this monastery and its worship periods were similar to Catholic monasteries, with sunrise, noontime, and sunset worship periods. The monk confirmed my hunch was correct. There would be a morning service and he told me to listen for the call to worship—drum and trumpet.

Before a dinner of rice, beans, potatoes, and some kind of meat, I stepped outside into the dusk and cold by myself to ponder Mount Everest and the monastery. Before me stood the Creator God Elohim's work of the Himalaya, and man's work of Tengboche Monastery to acknowledge the Creator of this range that was home to most of the planet's giant mountains.

The spiritual theme continued for me in another way as I thought about something one of our team members told me. He said another member of the team was carrying his late wife's ashes in hopes of having them blessed by one of the monastery's monks before he buried them somewhere on the trek. I didn't know the monks here. I did know from publications, videos, and emails that one or more monks did make themselves available to bless the climbers. I hoped they would address themselves to the man's wishes. What must be going through his mind, I wondered. "May he know God's mercy, peace, grace, and faith," I prayed. And, for myself, I wished I'd thought to ask for a monastic blessing for the journey while speaking to the monk.

At dinner Tom spoke about Trina, saying she was feeling sick and thinking of returning to Namche and waiting for us to return there on the way back from Base Camp. I was struck how these two, living in different parts of the big continent of Australia, remained close to each other as friends.

I stopped short of making a pastoral care visit to Trina. What was up with that? I am a hospital chaplain. Was I concerned about being too assertive—about getting too close to her? Well, whatever, I did tell Tom to let Trina know I was praying for her. I realized she did more than that for me at Namche. My bad.

After dinner Tom and I went outside, where it was now cold and dark, to ponder the stars. There were so many of them, they were so bright, and it seemed we could reach out and touch them. I turned to look at the monastery church, dim inside with traces of light here and there. I supposed that light comes from candles. This reminded me of St. Meinrad's Abbey Church at night. But here, off to the side, stood the white snow-capped peak of Everest.

The Buddhists believe their real God resides in these mountains. The ancient Jews believed the same of Zion and their real God, a site I've only seen in pictures. Mountain people of the Andes felt the same way.

Nearby, earlier in the light of day, I saw a kind of fenced graveyard, but not for human bodies. Rather it was a kind of above ground burial area for sacred stones that were cracked and broken. Worship stones called mani stones lie all along the trail to Everest. Cracked, broken, and discarded mani stone remained at rest in the "cemetery," where they were retired and piled up.

It was about 8 p.m., and so off to bed I went.

Saturday, 5 May, 2007

"Praise the Lord!" – an expression for this day, and also an act.

I am out of bed by 5:30 a.m., and dang it's cold in my tiny room. The door is only a few feet beyond my bed and twin beds wedged into this narrow space, with maybe two feet separating them. Each bed includes about a yard of storage space between the foot of the bed and the wall with the door. On the other end the beds are shoved up beside a poorly sealed window that lets cold air in. Hooks on the wall for hanging coats and clothes complete the Spartan amenities. I wonder if the other occupant of my room—a mouse behind the wall, considered his quarters cramped as he scrambled about behind the thin walls during the night.

Beyond my door is a short hallway leading to the community loo and an adjoining common area. We're sleeping indoors, but it's cold; very cold. Any heat we get comes from a fireplace in the common area, but there is no heat that I can discern. The thin exterior walls that barely protect us from the weather admit the cold, and perhaps the mice. The small window is a sieve for cold. Oh, well. I slept soundly and awakened at sunrise, as intended. I have plans before we push off on our day's trek.

The first thing I do is read some scripture by flashlight before leaving my warm sleeping bag. I'm already wearing polypropylene bottoms and top with warm socks and one layer of trekking clothes. When I stir from my cocoon sleeping bag I need only a few quick minutes to get dressed. I'm eager to get outside, wishing to take in the Himalayan range at sunrise, with a setting full moon gloriously shining above the tallest peaks on the planet. I intend to see the greater light, the sun, and the lesser light, the moon. I am expectant to see Chomolungma, Mother Goddess of Earth, while the mountain and I occupy the same area of the third planet, Earth. Then I will visit the monastery for morning worship, as I discussed yesterday with the monk.

Out of my room, I part the insulating doorway blankets aside, and push open the heavy wood door of our monastery grounds' lodge. Am I the only one outside just now? Well, my "community" this morning is nature. And nature is vividly present in its full regalia, soundless and richly stunning.

The morning moon hangs high over the left side of the mountain range, luminous and bright, nearly full as I behold its setting. It is white above white, the circular and cratered moon above the jagged mountains covered in their white mantle of glaciers and permanent snowfields. I am so transfixed I realize I forgot the greater light—the sun. I turn 180 degrees to see it. Whoa! I cannot yet see the sun's full orb. Instead, I see its dazzling rays radiating over the top of a mountain between us. The mountain is so tall it still has the planet eclipsed. I stand in the mountain's shade. Yet when I turn back to look again at the Himalaya, sunlight reaches the moon and the mountains. The sky is brilliantly blue, bluer than at home. I wonder if that's because we are at 12,600 feet and the air is thinner than southern Indiana's 600 feet of elevation. I hope my camera will record the true blueness as I saw it so vividly.

After meditating on the creative majesty of Elohim, "Creator God" in Hebrew, I walk to the monastery for morning worship. As noted by the monk, a trumpet sound comes from the monastery to break the silence of dawn. I expect this has been happening for a hundred some years, which reminds me to check the monastery's founding date. Yesterday the courtyard bustled with foreign trekkers going to worship, but at this hour it is empty. Well, there is a sacred cow in the courtyard, plus a dog. I admit myself through the ornate door, as I did yesterday, remembering to take off my boots. Brrrr! The stone floor is freezing cold.

Prayer already is under way—I hear chanting. I follow my steps of yesterday, hoping to sit where I did before. I smile, thinking there are people like me in every church who think their pew is *their pew* and get offended if someone else takes that seat." Well, "my seat" is wide open, close to the altar and all its man-made beauty. I am the only person who looks like me in attendance. This doesn't surprise me when I think about it. I am probably the only member of the trekker / climber community who has seminary experience and some feel for how a monastery operates. No one else knows or wishes to be here at sunrise unless they wear the purple and yellow robe of a monk.

Well, not to dwell on that. I am here for the sacred worship, for prayer, for praise of God and gratitude to Him as I know him, and to respect the monastics before me who know Him as they do. Our practice and our understanding may look and seem different. Yet, I agree with one of my teachers who said, "There's more that unites we people of faith than what separates us. Concentrate on what unites us rather than what separates us."

And so I listen to their words, which I don't understand. I observe their rituals, which I don't understand. What I understand is the reverence in how they conduct themselves this morning. I understand how important peace is to them, and how importantly they regard life. I understand how they, like Jewish families the world over, were run out of their homeland. In Tibet, hundreds of Buddhist monasteries were destroyed and thousands of monks and Tibetans killed by Chinese invaders about the time I was born. I marvel at this sacred place man has built, and rebuilt, and rebuilt again. I marvel at the setting in this extraordinary environment where the temple is located, perhaps more beautiful because it is so arduous to reach. I admire how these men have given themselves to God. And I offer my prayers with theirs, knowing that where two or more are gathered, we are promised God is present in their midst.

After some time in community worship, I stand, bow, and quietly excuse myself. I place some rupees in the collection box, put on my (now cold) trek boots, and thank God for his place at the center of my life. I also thank him for this faith community and that I was part of it for a while.

I leave the monastery feeling vibrant and alive, although walking on chilly feet. I worshipped this morning in the great natural cathedral of the Himalayan Mountains with God's magnificent nature surrounding me, and then I worshipped within a man-made structure with a community that is rich in peace, in tradition, in faith. Talk about vibrant and alive.

After attending services at the monastery, hot tea and hot oatmeal taste good and warm me all the way to my cold toes. Back on the trail to Everest Base Camp, we do a three hour morning trek to the village of Pangboche. Three things struck me: The unbelievable load a small-size Sherpa carried, signs for one of the famous Hillary-built primary schools, and two bicyclists on the trail.

Now we were steadily ascending hundreds and sometimes a thousand and more feet each day. The trail sometimes went up fairly steep inclines although usually steps were somehow cut into the existing rock or built into the trail. However, these steps were uneven and varied greatly in height from one step to the next. Some could be 12 to 14 inches high. Because the steps often lacked a flat stepping surface, this could be tricky when carrying a 25 pound backpack. And sometimes people went both ways, so we sometimes had to stop to let people going down mountain pass by first. And always the yaks went first. Their wide bodies and even wider span of horns meant we had to stand well off to the side. The yak didn't mean any harm—they simply knew only to go forward or stop. The unwary traveler could be trampled, gored, or both. Beware the yak!

I did fairly well with my backpack, despite some soreness in my shoulders during the first few days. I helped myself with strap adjustment and reloading the pack's contents to get things better balanced. I also took Ibuprofen, and applied Bengay topical cream and I'd usually be ready to go in the mornings. Some of our group, who hadn't trained well, found themselves with more issues carrying a pack. How the Sherpas carried packs or loads that must've weighed 50 to 80 or more pounds was beyond me. Some carried boxes of beer strapped to their back. Others carried open straw baskets filled to the brim with freshly butchered meat (probably from the shop in Namche). The meat was stacked in the basket with no wrapping. Some loads seemed unbalanced and unwieldy.

No roads in these mountains—I never heard the sound of a truck engine. Everything that went up the mountain was hauled by yaks or on people's backs, and most often that meant Sherpas shouldered the burden. A few cargo helicopters flew the mountain, but seldom flew above Namche. In fact, in a few days we would see a crashed chopper at Base Camp. The air was too thin for the rotor blades to get bite and lift and stay in the air. The newest choppers could make Base Camp, but it was still risky. In fact on that day we observed a chopper heading there and returning. When I ask Dorzee about this, he said he'd heard a climber was critically injured or killed. Oh, my prayers around that.

With this for backdrop, imagine the sight I beheld.

I was 5'7' tall and weighed 167 pounds when I left for Nepal. Along the trail I saw a Sherpa lad, perhaps in his early 20s, who appeared less than five feet tall and probably weighed 140 pounds. This porter carried a load of cut timber 15 feet long that measured about three inches by four inches.

I know the dimensions because at a stop when he was unloaded I stepped off the distance of the load to size up its length, and eyeballed the rest. I estimated the weight at 100 pounds. And 15 feet in length made for an unbalanced and unwieldy load on any man, let alone one of his height and weight.

Yet, this young man was so strong he and his big load passed us at our next break. Unbelievably, he reached the next village before we did. The strength of the Sherpas is incredible. Incidentally, Sherpa is not a job title. Sherpas are a people native to that part of Nepal and the word Sherpa means "people from the east," referring to ancestral Sherpas. They migrated to the so-named Khumbu region of Nepal, the mountainous geographic area around Everest, from Tibet and environs, located to the east. The Sherpas who accompanied us were born and raised in these mountains, descended from many generations of Himalayan mountain people. They adapted to this elevation and terrain over centuries. These strong, resourceful people have been supporting expeditions to Everest since foreigners, first the English, then the Swiss, began coming here in the early 1900s.

The porter of the wooden beams clearly caught my attention. What respect I had for him, and by extension for our porter crew and the four Nepalese who led our expedition. Perhaps because of my age, I especially liked Dorzee (pronounced Door-g), and Saila

(Say-lah) who were closer in age to me. I also enjoyed Rame (said Ramish) and Razkumar (Rah-jud) their younger counterparts. I expect the latter were being mentored by the senior guides.

As if the young porter of the lumber wasn't amazing enough, something I saw a bit later was in part curious, part adventure, and all amazing. I am a bicyclist who has ridden mileage equivalent to more than twice around the world (60,000+ miles) in nine consecutive years. This feat was accomplished just before my interest in climbing mountains began. And my son Andy loves to ride his bicycle off-road up and down forest trails in and around Brown County State Park near where he and wife Jill live. That's not for me. I like to bike smoothly paved roads.

The attention getter I mentioned was all about off-road biking, and distance. It had absolutely zero to do with smooth surfaces. As we climbed our next set of uneven steps, on the trail at the top I saw two guys standing alongside bicycles. I rubbed my eyes in disbelief. They didn't speak English. Soon I had a closer look at two sturdy road bikes and the stalwart young men beside them.

I heard they had just ridden 35 plus miles to Base Camp and were now returning. They pedaled their bikes where they could and pushed or carried the bikes where they couldn't pedal. They seemed accustomed to the stares and attention the sight of them commanded. I wondered if they rode across the high bridge over the river gorge into Namche. I wondered if Andy would dare ride that bridge. No thanks, not me. The roughest road I ever bicycled was Guanella Pass through the Sawtooth Ridge above Georgetown, Colorado, while visiting my friend Marge. What these guys were riding made me think the rough roadbed I rode on through the Guanella Pass was a super highway.

The third thing that gave me pause was a sign—a simple sign, hand-lettered in perfect penmanship, pointing the way to:

Pangboche Primary School, established by Sir Edmund Hillary, 1963. Sir Ed was the first summiteer of Everest along with Sherpa Tenzing Norgay, ten years before that school was built. A great humanitarian to the Sherpa people, Hillary returned to Everest numerous times. On one of his first climbing trips after Everest, having come to know many Sherpas as friends, he asked how he might repay all the kindnesses accorded him. Their answer was, "Could you build us a little school." Hillary's return trips resulted in 50 some school buildings, medical clinics, and a hospital.

A beekeeper from New Zealand who was knighted by the crown, Sir Ed always said what he did building schools and medical facilities was much more important than his summit. He raised hundreds of thousands of dollars to buy materials to build the schools. Now deceased, he remains a hero to the Sherpa people.

On one of the trips a plane crash in the Everest area tragically claimed the lives of his wife and daughter. I hope Sir Ed was the recipient of grief support like Wings for the Journey which I facilitate for bereft parents. Later I would see one of the schools he built. Have you ever been asked, "Who in the world would you most like to have lunch with?" Sir Ed is at the top of my list.

After our team's lunch, more starchy stuff ala rice and potato, and fish that tasted, looked, and smelled like it came straight from a can, I visited with Tom. We spoke of the morning's events and our callings at home.

Our group went on a two hour acclimatizing hike that took us above 14,000 feet of elevation. My PR or personal record elevation was 14,500 so I was getting close. I had no headache, or any other aches; I felt good. Trina had resumed the hike and said she was feeling better. My appetite remained healthy, and when I checked the waistband of my pants I figured I hadn't lost any weight. That night I went to be about 8 p.m. and awakened about 5 a.m.

Sunday, 6 May, 2007

Mother's Day (or so I thought)

"Happy Mother's Day" I said to my mom, who is deceased. Yet, I felt confident she heard me loud and clear from heaven and smiled at my greeting. Mom's hearing on earth was compromised by working many second shift stints as an Indiana Bell Telephone operator wearing an early generation headset. While a hearing aid helped in her later years, I suspect her hearing is perfect in heaven. I also sent wishes too to Aunt Angie, who helped my mom raise me and my brother.

In addition, I said a prayer for the mother of my children, Dom and Andy. This caused me to think about Dom, Kathryn, and Andy. I missed them all the more.

After I returned home from Everest, I realized Mother's Day was the second Sunday in May, not the first. My journal entries, came a week ahead of time. Better early than late!

That morning as I prepared to head for the loo, I experienced a toilet paper shortage. Did one of those mountain monster yetis break into my pack and steal my essential paper? I laughed at myself, hoping this was a case of misplacement inside my back pack. St. Anthony is the patron of things lost in the Catholic tradition, so he became my go-to guy for the MIA toilet paper. I smiled, thinking, "I wonder if this is his first request to find toilet paper."

While preparing for the day's trek, I also remembered it was time for the Indianapolis Mini Marathon. I had completed 50 mini marathons, half in Indianapolis and half in Louisville, since my home in Columbus is almost exactly midway between the two starting lines. I had only missed one race since I started running. The day ahead of me would be a three hour hike. I used to run the mini of 13.1 miles in 2 hours, but there would be no running for me in this thin air, with trek boots and a backpack.

From Pangboche we hiked toward Dingboche, crossing above the tree line, which was the last vegetation we would see until our inbound return. The air was now too thin, with too little oxygen, for vegetation to grow. At lunch I spent time with a guy from Boulder, Colorado who was traveling with another group that also planned to overnight at Dingboche. I was familiar with Colorado, having skied there for 30 consecutive years. We chatted each other up about the state. His reason for visiting Everest intrigued me. He was, he told me, the IMAX director for the sequel to the award winning Everest film by IMAX in 1996, when 10 people died on the mountain amid heroic rescues. He said he was headed to the summit of Everest, where he'd been before, this time with a combined Brit and American expedition. He mentioned on-mountain clinical examinations around blood and urine testing. These would also include stationary exercise bicycles to determine acclimatization aspects of humans. I remembered reading about this on everestnews.com and understood it was called off by the Nepalese government because the testing was to include Sherpas. The government, which issues the permits to climb Everest, had some ethical considerations.

Mr. Boulder was certainly friendly and talkative, but he made me wonder which of us had our facts right. We went our separate ways as I had some chores to attend to. This was an interesting encounter, yet I felt unsettled as to facts. My intuition waved a red flag. Months later I still hadn't seen the IMAX sequel he mentioned. Had it in fact opened and I missed it? Maybe it didn't happen—cancelled perhaps. But I also wondered if Mr. Boulder was having fun stretching the truth with me. And why? Ah, what did I know? I let it go.

Note: These pages were edited in autumn 2015—the same time the new movie *Everest* was released. My publisher wondered if the man was referring to this new movie. I attended a presentation by renown mountaineer and cinematographer David Beshears who had a hand in its making. So I asked him. "No," he said.

Two more interesting things occurred before bedtime: I washed my clothes in a freezing stream, with water gushing from a hose that flowed directly from the Khumbu Icefall. My hands felt almost frostbitten from doing laundry. Where's the Guinness Book of World Records people when you need them? I could be a medical first!

Intrigued by the conversation with Mr. Boulder, I had questions for each member of our crew. I asked just about everyone about their age, height, and weight. If clinicians were around to gather blood workups, body mass index, blood pressures, temperatures, scientific data, and medical history, this would have been more informative gathering of demographic data. But the general information made for an interesting picture, though unscientific. For our group minus "the Aussie kids" who would have skewed the age median lower, the findings were:

a) Average age was 44,

b) Average height was 5'6," and

c) Average weight was 144 pounds.

By our group's standards, I was:

a) Senior at age 58;

b) Average within the height mean at 5'7," and

c) Heavy at 167.

However, I felt great: A + for that.

At dinner I was reminded that lately rice and potatoes always showed up on our plates and sometimes even at dinner eggs were served. Tea was always in the cups. And it all seemed to pretty much taste the same.

I spoke at length to Trina about the loss of her late husband. I hoped what I said provided pastoral care that gave her solace. I hoped my listening was non-judgmental and helpful.

Immediately after dinner I went off to bed, hoping for another good sleep. And I hoped Trina would also sleep well.

Monday 7, May, 2007

I awakened about 5 a.m. and watched the sunrise reveal the beautiful, pyramidic shape of Amadablam, one of the most picturesque mountains in the Himalaya, indeed in the world. It is one of the 10 highest peaks on this planet. Thanks to Ramish our junior trek guide, I now have an oil painting of the peak hanging in my home. Turns out he is an accomplished artist.

The teahouse had such paper thin walls I could clearly hear sleeping bag zippers sliding next door and people speaking in low sounds, just above a whisper, with accents of UK and US. I wondered if they were part of the UK and US medical acclimatization study and IMAX movie project Mr. Boulder spoke of yesterday.

In three more days, God willing, we would reach Everest Base Camp. Dorzee noticed I was red faced from the sun and instructed me, "Put on more sunscreen, and wear your hat the right way!" Busted! I thought I was using enough sunscreen, but obviously not. And wearing my ball cap backwards to get some rays did not help matters. But here at 14,000 feet I should've been smarter. The air is thin and ultra violet waves strike and stick on skin with more intensity.

This day brought another acclimatizing hike of 2.5 hours. And it was a tall one. I notched a personal record of 15,700 feet in elevation, well above my 14,500 mark while skiing in Chile when

I got the lift from a chopper. Praise the Lord and rock and roll. However, I went a little fuzzy for a moment as I looked about while walking, looking up, down, and back up too quickly. Note to self—control head and eye movements.

The village of Chukhung was our destination, and we saw many of the Himalayan Mountain Range wonders: Island Peak, Amadablam, Makalu, Lohtse, and Everest. Well, Everest was shy and shrouded in clouds. Except for my momentary fogginess, which matched the clouds in the area, I felt good. As a matter of fact, most of our party did well.

However, two members of our group stayed back at the monastery, where they decided to bag it there and await our return. The married couple, Eddie and Ron, held up. Actually, as I understood it, one of them thought it best to withdraw and in a show of support the other held up as well. It sounded like a good decision by the first to be safe, and a thoughtful decision by the second who, even though he believed he could make it, decided to hold up, also.

Word circulated from those in another group to our group that the weather on Everest was "heavy," accounting perhaps for the cloud cover we experienced on this day. This reminded me to say the Weather Prayer, and I did so. I would feel disappointed to get this far and have a change in the weather scuttle our journey to Base Camp.

On returning to our lodge, I went to the dining area to get refreshment and write in my journal. There I met a man from Aspen, CO named Martin, sitting a few tables away. His keen eyesight noted the red journal I was writing in, a gift from Snowmass Ski Resort, one of the Aspen destination ski areas. The journal was a nice Christmas marketing gift, suitable and timely for my purposes. Thank you, Snowmass. Martin, some tables away said something to me I didn't quite hear. I didn't know if he were speaking to me. He was looking my way and he spoke again, but I still couldn't hear. Then, he held up a little book he was writing in, and I saw a little red journal exactly like mine. Too cool. I popped up from my chair and headed his way.

He waved the book as I reached him and said, "Snowmass! I saw yours too." We shook hands and had a delightful conversation. He knew of John Russell, the famous Aspen photographer who grew up in my town and whose hospitality I enjoyed at his family home. John's brother George and family live in Columbus and George and Judy's sons and my sons are good friends.

I knew of an Aspen connection to Everest, so I asked Martin if he knew the brothers who were planning to ski down Cho Oyu, a neighbor mountain of Everest, after they climbed it. I had followed their exploits on everstnews.com before departing for Nepal myself. He knew of them and updated me to say they did summit the mountain and then skied down it. Holy moley, I thought. Climbing a huge Himalayan mountain and then skiing down. Imagine that!

We spoke of skiing at Snowmass, and I told him. "My favorite area is Hanging Valley Wall," referring to a back country access area.

Martin nodded knowingly, then frowned. "Yep. Climbing up and across the mountain, carrying your skis on your shoulder to get to it. Far out," Martin said. "But no more."

"What do you mean?" I asked in disbelief.

"The ski resort operators built a lift to Hanging Valley."

"Oh, no!" I winced.

Instantly, I remembered seeing the Snowmass Master Plan and realized it was carried out. The lift had been on the resort's drawing board and they finally implemented the plan.

"Bummer," I told Martin. "For two reasons: I loved that back country because so few people made it there, and everyone earned it by carrying their skis up and over the ridge."

He nodded in agreement.

Refreshed by tea and a delightful visit with Martin that invoked pleasant memories, I headed back outside to reunite with our group. It was mid-afternoon, with the sun shining. I strolled over to where some of our group were seated on the courtyard, leaning up against a building. I found an empty spot and joined them. I sat facing the sun like a day at the beach. Beach, yeah, right. We were at almost 16,000 feet.

As an afterthought, I checked the adjustment of my hat to keep the sun off my face. So much for the beach.

Tom sat next to me and I began a conversation, but he said, "Shhh," and nodded toward the courtyard in front of us. Basking in the sunlight, happy from my conversation with Martin and thinking of mutual friends and family in Indiana and Aspen, and all the fun I had skiing at Snowmass, for a moment I was oblivious to our surroundings. Tom stilled me because of an escalating argument between two people standing in the middle of the courtyard in front of us. They pointed fingers at each other and their voices were rising. Given the intensity, I quickly realized those pointed fingers could close into fists.

The manager of the inn where we were staying and a vendor supplying him with product saw things differently on prices, the quantity of product supplied, and what had been paid for. I watched the two posture for a while and finally decided I wasn't interested. I didn't need to know how this would play out. Thinking of Martin, I pulled out my red book and resumed journaling, ignoring the quarrel before us. Mindful of Tom's rebuke, I quietly let those who wanted to watch the life drama do so. If the two combatants finally shook hands, I missed it, but their feud eventually died down and peace was restored.

At dinner I had a bit of panic because my eyes developed a burning sting. What's up with this?" I wondered? The pain and itching was so intense I could barely keep my eyes open. Though I tried not to, I rubbed them, which brought momentary relief but seemed to make them continue stinging. Noticing my distress, Dorzee, my pastoral care chaplain from Namche, asked a few diagnostic questions. He then brought steaming warm water in a bowl, a blanket that had probably been pulled from one of the cargo yaks, judging by its smell, and constructed a makeshift vapor tent at the table in the dining room. The treatment slowly worked and my panic and fear of the unknown subsided as the stinging went away. "Thank you, God, for Dorzee, my medicine man and chaplain."

Tuesday, 8 May, 2007

A headline awaited my eyes as I slipped out of my cozy bag to take a frosty leak in a teahouse that had little heat. I awakened to an overnight snowfall, the remnant of weather we'd heard about. From a hallway window next to the loo, I looked at the courtyard where yesterday's antagonists argued. The courtyard was empty at dawn, of course, but the clothesline was full—and there was my headline. The clothesline was full, with snow piled atop a-top all the clothes on the line. You read it here first:

I recorded in my journal: "Never saw that before in my 59 years of life! Happy that isn't my underwear! Putting those on would get your anatomy in a wad ! Glad I brought my clothes in!"

I knew snow was not in the forecast for Indiana, because this day was the running of the Indianapolis 500—The Greatest Spectacle in Racing. Wait, that couldn't be right. This was Tuesday. With the time differential the race must have been held the previous day. No the day before. Whatever. I definitely missed it. We were 10.25 hours ahead of Indiana. Yes, you read that right. Something about the curvature of the earth bends this time zone.

Anyway, I attended plenty of races as a young person, but these days I rarely go to the famed track. I still listen in on race day, just as I used to do on radio before I saw the 33 cars fly around the oval and sometimes crash in front of my very own eyes.

Thoughts of the 500 Mile Race blended with the snowy clothes on the line. That day's goal would be Lobuche at 16,200 feet. Then, the following day was our dream shot—Mount Everest Base Camp. But I tried not to get ahead of myself. I needed to perform well every day. Hydrate. "Be safe," as my dear friend Kit Klingelhoffer counseled me before I left. And I wanted to appreciate all the special moments along the way.

A significant moment awaited us that morning at the top of a long and tall hill we continuously climbed for 50 minutes. Ben led our group half-way up the incline, then I led for a while. Finally, Sailah took us to the top, the last stretch being the steepest. Afterward, we felt tuckered out. We'd gone up and up for a long time and I felt breathless in the thin air. We had periodic sunlight during the morning, but as we neared the top of this forever hill the weather became socked in, as though we were walking into a cloud. Perhaps that was nature's way of saying– "You are entering holy ground." And so we had.

The top of the hill held a level plateau with a kind of cemetery the size of a soccer field, with many cairns and mani stones. These were memorials to Sherpas and non-sherpas who died climbing Everest. Mani stones are rocks chiseled and painted with religious symbols and messages. The cairns were memorials constructed of little and big rocks, laid and fitted together and atop each other. Some were four and five feet tall.

I recognized one with a dedicatory plaque for Scott Fischer. I knew his story. An American, he led one of two expeditions caught in a fierce snow storm high on Everest in 1996. Tragically, he was one of ten climbers who died in a storm that made international headlines as the worst day ever at that time, on the notoriously unforgiving mountain.

I showed Mike, the Jewish man, the memorial to "A Child of Israel" from Dallas whose memorial had the Star of David carved on it. He thanked me and took note of the name.

The clouds remained and I thought this seemed fitting. Nature engulfed us in a sacred shroud that we might go slowly and remember the men and women, primarily Sherpas, who died climbing the mountain. Some of the cairns carried no names. Many were adorned with prayer flags.

We rested for a bit to recover from the steep climb to the memorial ground, which was a tough stretch. Reflecting, I believed I'd climbed well so far, only resting momentarily on the hill. My heartbeat returned to its resting rate shortly after I gained level ground at the top of the hill. I was now wearing gloves, a headband, and the blue, heavy, down puffy jacket (actually my second day for the big coat). The weather was cold and windy.

The wind increased as we returned to the trail and ascended a long gradual steppe. Suddenly I heard a piercing voice. Wait, it was two voices speaking in German, loud enough to carry above the wind, and we were uphill from them walking into that wind. They were probably within earshot for ten minutes before they overtook and passed us.

During the minute or two they were alongside our group, I had a delightful surprise. Despite their conversational racket, it was Johan the Swede whom I visited with at Tengboche and his Base Camp manager whom I'd also met. Johan's speed and giant stride carried him past us quickly—but not before the two of us made eye contact and exchanged a nod of remembrance. Days later, according to everestnews.com, he would successfully ascend Mt. Everest.

Later I heard one of the big talkers in our group scorn the loud, boisterous conversation of these two men who passed us on the trail. The critic was someone who for days now, in a voice often decibels higher than was necessary, had a lot to say as we trekked. Now this person complained, whining out loud, "I wish those guys would shut up."

I smiled to myself, thinking, "If only you knew how *your* jabbering disturbs me. Take a little of your own medicine. Learn from it, please." Of course, I also considered this was their trip too and recalled my "advice to self" about neither separating from people, nor rebuking them. What was it Supreme Court Justice Learned Hand said? "My right to swing my fist ends where my fellow man's nose begins."

As Johan passed and we nodded, I said, "Hello Johan from Sweden," cheerily. Recognizing me, he gave me a big smile and said, "Hello. Do well!"

A strange and unsettling thing happened after we reached Lobuche, our final overnight before striking out the next morning for Base Camp. Near our lodgings, one of our group, perhaps moved by the cemetery sights earlier, decided to bury the cremains of a family member he carried with him. Word circulated about the burial as if we are all to attend in support. I and the others prepared to go, and I told him I'd be right along. To my surprise and dismay, he responded, "You can't come. You're not invited."

I had been rejected, and had no idea why. I think others were excluded too, or perhaps they just excused themselves. Unbeknown to me, I had apparently offended someone I thought I was getting along with. Well, maybe I didn't offend him. But for whatever reason I was not included. I felt surprised, but it was his ceremony. I did my best to let this go and to use my time wisely by photographing some teeny-tiny blue and purple flowers near the trail that otherwise seemed to resemble pictures of a Martian or lunar landscape. The land was arid and dry—not unlike the emotional landscape I experienced after this rejection.

Just away from the trail I spotted a patch of green amid a pile of boulders. The ground felt a little soupy underfoot there and I thought I could hear a spring gurgling. Oh, my gosh. The circulating water underground produced a dramatic little garden. I snapped pictures of it and also got photos of yaks peacefully resting and grazing nearby, untethered, not even hobbled. Thinking of the flowers' beauty and the animals' stillness and contentedness helped center me, and I regained my own peace—for a time.

My camera and memory recorded scenes of life before me, while somewhere nearby a ritual for the dead took place, as nature's cyclic ritual gave and took life. I have been blessed to conduct a number of funerals.

Such times invite and require sensitivity to the bereaved and to family. On this day I respected the right of a family member to invite to a service those he wanted—and exclude those he didn't want. Yet, to be honest—I was hurt. I thought I was friends with the bereft person, so I didn't see this coming. Nonetheless, I could and did offer prayers of support.

I focused on studying the yaks that seemed to flourish at high elevations. Their thick, dense wool is prized as the warmest of woolen materials because it protects these beasts who roam at high elevations, typically not descending below 10,000 feet. There's a story about a yak and a water buffalo who were friends and lived at lower elevation in the foothills. They both loved salt, but little was available where they roamed. The yak said to his friend, "Lend me your long warm hair and I will walk to Tibet and find salt for us." The water buffalo thought this was a good idea and complied. The yak went off wearing the warm hair and never returned. He liked the high altitudes, the wind and the snow. The buffalo's thick, dense warm hair kept him warm. Lo these many centuries later, according to the legend, the buffalo, shivering and hungry, still keeps watch and wonders when the yak will return with his hair and his salt.

Later, when I was in my tea house room journaling, the man who dis-invited me to the committal service stopped by. "You didn't go up to the ridge," he said.

"I wasn't invited," I said flatly looking him straight in the eye, and holding the eye contact.

"I was joking," he said.

I offered no response and I held the eye contact.

"That was the hardest thing I've ever done," he responded.

My pastoral care side softened me as I expected he would talk about the emotional toll associated with burying the ashes. Surprising me again, he went the other direction and instead spoke about the physical exertion of a tough climb to a spot. And then he left.

In a new fog, denser than the one at the memorial grounds, I asked myself, "What was up with that? What just happened? Was it his way of trying to make peace? If he didn't want me to go, why did he stop now and ask why I didn't go? What was up with the exclusion, which sounded perfectly absolute and negative when it was spoken?" I had no idea what just occurred.

Then I remembered the resting yaks and the flowers. I also remembered the story of the water buffalo who still waited for the yak. There are times we live with mysteries—hopefully in peace. We can grouse about it and struggle to find answers. Or we can sit with ambiguity, in peace. It is a choice. I have learned the world is gray, not black and white. To be accepting of ambiguity without pressing for an answer can be freeing.

I would control what I could control and let go of everything else. I cannot dwell on that which I cannot. Tomorrow would be the final stretch to Everest Base Camp, so I needed all my wits and energy about me. Focus was essential. Maybe what just happened would one day make sense. I did not push for an explanation. I wished to let this go, and I did so.

Mr. Boulder resurfaced and we chatted for a bit. Remembering Martin from Aspen, I mentioned him. Boulder knew Martin, he said. As Boulder and I visited, he told me he'd summited Everest four times. Holy Moley! Really, I wondered? He hoped this one would be his last and said that 30 or more expeditions were on the mountain this season.

"Has anyone summited yet?" I asked.

He said he though one or more Sherpas who were fixing rope had done so. Those fixing rope high up the mountain in dangerous terrain are known as "ice doctors." These talented Sherpas are the first ones into the danger zone at the beginning of each climbing season. They risk limb and life to fix ladders and ropes in the Khumbu Icefall where so many of Everest's deaths occur when towers of ice crash down on Sherpas, and on men and women climbers without warning. The ice doctors prepare, or "fix," safety or climbing ropes and ladders much of the way to the top, and in doing so often record the first summits. The work is lucrative and deadly.

We were 1,400 feet below the prize of Everest Base Camp. Lobuche stands at 16,200 feet and the air turned freezing cold as the sun faded. Most people added extra clothes. From nine, our group now numbered seven, plus our four Sherpas. I looked around the room as dinner was served and wondered if all of us, including me, would reach Base Camp. I fully knew that was my intention and felt confident in my preparations. At dinner, I didn't feel hungry. This was strange, but I didn't think much about it. I believed the lack of appetite was caused by my excitement about the next day when, God willing, I would fulfill an adventurous dream. I wasn't then as mature in my faith as I would become. I didn't ask the group if I might offer a prayer for the day before us, but I did pray quietly for me and for all of us, including the guy who buried the cremains.

Something had happened to me apart from the cremains incident. No alarm bells went off to signal this. What escaped my notice was something I should have been keenly aware of. I didn't eat much at dinner that night. Normally I had a voracious appetite and consistently belonged to the "Clean Plate Club" except perhaps when I had the upset GI tract. I was teased with the outdated saw about being on a "see-food diet," because I ate everything in sight. Not on this night, however.

That was Sign One. And I missed it. Instead, I was thinking of the words on one of the cairns in the memorial garden: "Aim High." My stomach didn't feel upset. I just wasn't hungry and failed to recognize this sign for what it was.

Wednesday, 9 May, 2007

This was the big day and we rose early for the trek to Mount Everest Base Camp—my dream about to come true. However, bad news and good news greeted me.

Sign Two came during the night, and I missed this one also. Although I slept like a little boy almost every night on this trip, I felt restless that night—all night long. I thought I couldn't sleep because of excitement about Base Camp. All those nights of wonderful sleep, and now I couldn't rest. But then again—how often does one trek to Everest Base Camp?

My morning started with a surprise, a pleasant one that had nothing to do with the signs that began appearing. The man who upset and confused me with his actions about the cremains approached me first thing at breakfast, walking right over to where I was seated.

"I'm sorry for yesterday," he said.

I looked up at him. He seemed serious and sincere. I realized there was no point using language or comments to judge him or make a rebuke. This was no time for questions. There was one thing to do as the man offered his apology. I put out my hand to shake his. "I accept your apology," I said, "and I appreciate it."

When we shook hands, I saw this as a positive way to begin a huge day. Having prayed about the division between the two of us, and having let go of it were the best things I could have done. Look at how this turned out. I was grateful I didn't spend energy trying to analyze the bereft man's behavior. Some things we shouldn't require all the answers about. Besides, the man struck me as being sincere. He did something many people cannot conceive of—he apologized. And for myself, I hoped I was becoming more mature about not judging.

The whole episode was an epiphany.

The man and I never discussed it again. But the rewind of reflection in the days ahead brought it round to me again. As we had steadily made our climb, earlier, somewhere in the miles of words, in a conversation, this same man taught me about "the duty of care." Simply, I learned from him, it is a person's responsibility, his or her obligation, to render care to one who is in need. This standard doesn't suggest, but requires, one go to the aid of another, no matter who that person is.

I knew of this practice handed down from Judeo-Christian ancients who extended themselves and bent their backs to help, typically, their tribal kin—people they knew or were related to. Then from the New Testament emerged the bar-setting story where a Samaritan, a dis-respected stranger, on a trek of his own like us, did what even the respected locals of his area avoided. He stretched to help someone not of his own kin. He bent his own back, spent his own money, and cared for a man beaten by robbers. He treated and bound the wounds of a man he didn't know and was not related to. The Samaritan put the robbery victim on his own donkey, ferried him to an inn, paid for his bed and board, and directed that he be cared for. The Samaritan told the innkeeper if additional charges were rung up, he'd settle with the innkeeper on his return journey.

The good Samaritan's actions were noble indeed and the story Jesus told about him is recorded in the gospels as an example of duty of care. My question is: Did the Samaritan feel obliged to care for a stranger avoided by locals who passed by? Or was he compassion-driven? I think the answer is, the compassion he felt toward the nameless stranger produced an environment of wanting to help. The word "obligation" implies one has to do whatever needs to be done. Love, on the other hand is a word, a feeling, and an action higher than law. When we act out of love for another, as opposed to duty, that action is on a higher level than obligation. Either way, the one in need is cared for.

I had never considered the "obligation" of such circumstances. At Everest, back then, I believed it to be a compassion-driven intuition or notion that motivated, that drove one to help, taught by principles handed down by parents and ancestors. Some people did it, like the Samaritan. Others didn't—like those who walked past the beaten man in the gospel story.

My own study of Everest portrayed heroic climbers who abandoned their own dreams and climbed to help someone in trouble on the mountain. This was the Everest gold standard of this teaching. This was all about surrender and subordination—putting the needs of others ahead of self. As an authentic human being, the man who apologized gave some of his care to me. I remain grateful to him for it. Did he feel obliged out of duty of care, or out of compassion, for another, for me, to so behave? I cannot say.

Of course, all this came later. I didn't consider as I was courting euphoria—and disaster—with the trek to Everest Base Camp before me and its prize only hours away.

Sign Three is another one I missed. I didn't eat much at breakfast, just as I hadn't eaten the previous night. Eggs and some oatmeal or porridge-like something or other was in front of us on the table. We didn't see the protein of meat or fish up this high. The food was, as I remember, moderately warm and the tea was hot. Thankfully, the common room where we ate had a stove—the only one for the entire building, including our sleeping spots. However, the room was cool to cold, despite the stove. Many of us already wore much of the warm and protective clothing we'd be wearing outside within a few minutes.

Back to Sign Three: Cumulatively, on the fuel side, I was experiencing deficits. I had eaten little in the last 12 hours. Along with that, I slept little. I had before me a grueling, uphill 4.5 hour trek to Base Camp—and that would come after we reached Gorak Shep, still a couple of hours away.

That I overlooked or dismissed the warning signals of these signs was Sign Four. I was oblivious, showing slippage in the area of critical thinking. Ah, but euphoria overrides disaster. It was time to head out to Base Camp. Hoo-ray! I knew these final seven hours would be anything but a walk in the park, and I was respectful of the mountain and its dangers, but I had modest self-confidence from all my training in Hoosier land. I felt prepared. And I'd been successful in my experience so far on the mountain trek. Tsk, tsk, tsk—it should have been obvious ... my euphoria trumpeted a pending near-disaster.

Clarity would have made me aware of signals, with alarm bells ringing. No such good fortune. Thin air and its cognitive deficits hijacked my ability to think straight.

We began our trek to Everest Base Camp in a snowfall, with intermittent freezing rain. Word passed up the line as we trekked that Ingrid had dropped out early. Dang, too bad. I hoped she was okay. I'd have to check with Deckland at our break. I really liked Ingrid and Deckland and had been spending more time with "the kids" than with anyone. Now our party had dwindled to six, plus our Sherpas.

We moved at a steady pace, leaving footprints in the snow as our line headed toward Gorak Shep, the last outpost before Everest Base Camp. We would have an early lunch at Gorak Shep, still some four hours below Base Camp.

By the time we got there, I felt sleepy and tired. This I recognized. While awaiting brunch I tried to take a power nap in my booth, just leaning back. We were so close, I don't want to falter. More than that, I wanted to be at my best. My power nap fizzled—I still couldn't sleep.

When brunch arrived, I thought, "Cripes, more soup, rice, potatoes, and eggs." We hadn't seen meat for three or four meals, or was it three or four days? We had a few servings of canned tuna here and there, but the food was exceedingly bland it seemed to me. Again, I ate litte—Sign Five. Still, I didn't catch on.

Appetites do wane at high altitudes. But climbers know they must eat to have strength, and when they're thinking clearly, or being watched over by another person, they do so. A failing of our leadership was that we were not assigned trek partners to watch one another's behaviors. No one noticed I wasn't eating. Soon I wouldn't be drinking the amount of water I should, yet another critical sign of absent clarity and that I was headed for trouble.

We left Gorak Shep, four hours below Base Camp. "Oh, my God—almost there!" I told myself. We had hiked and climbed steadily since daybreak. After our early lunch, or lack of it in my case, it was mid-morning. We were at 17,000 feet. I had never been this high. And though we would ascend only 600 feet higher, we had several linear miles to trek.

The first thing we did was cross a large dry lake bed. The rocks underfoot were unstable and tended to roll beneath our feet. Right away I could tell my steps were unsure as I moved from one wobbly rock to the next. I stumbled a few times and immediately knew that wasn't good. Still, I had yet to connect the dots of the previous signs. I ascribed my clumsiness to lack of sleep. And that certainly played into the equation, but the fact that I didn't put all the pieces together was telling. Thankfully, I got across the dry lake bed and onto terra firma of the trail, solid ground underfoot.

As we trekked I thought, "Surely Base Camp can't be too far now. We've been going for a long time." I was wrong about that.

We ascended a rocky section of trail and as it leveled out my foot caught the top of a rock and I stumbled forward, falling down. I was unhurt and only horizontal for a moment. That was my first fall on the entire expedition. I got up and dusted myself off.

My clumsiness in the dry lake bed, and now the stumble, were different than all my trekking and ascending during the expedition to that point. I had another sobering setback in a little bit when I lost my balance and fell backward at a rest stop. My steps and pace had been confident and sure, steady, with no bobbles or stumbles.

I managed the tough sections without pause, felt good about my work, and received compliments from Dorzee, and others. So I lulled myself into thinking I was just tired from lack of sleep. As for the rest of the group, either no one noticed that morning's sloppy performance, or they chose not to comment.

We gained a ridge and for the first time up close, I saw the Khumbu Glacier flowing through a deep gorge it had carved on my right. I heard occasional sounds like gunfire and cannon I remembered from my military days. But this noise was the frozen river of ice slowly inching forward in its movement, receiving propulsion from the disintegrating Khumbu Icefall breaking up above Base Camp, and then slowly descending downward. The ice in the gorge was blue-green in color in the sections where it wasn't white or milky gray. I mostly kept my eyes on the trial, which grew narrow here. One false step to the right and I would fall 100 feet toward the danger of those sounds and colors.

"No stumbles now, Wal. Pick up your feet. Every step. Watch where you step," I told myself. I think this message was the "C" of caution borne of fear from what I saw, not the "C" of clarity. No matter. The message was valid and clear.

We dropped down to the left and maybe 50 yards ahead I saw Sailah stopping others of our group. From time to time he would release one, and then another, to go forward. One at a time. Then another. Had I been thinking right I might have counted the seconds, or my steps, or some way of getting the rhythm of what he was doing. Another of our guides waited farther ahead along the trail, a half football field and more away. I wondered what was up. On reaching Sailah, he pointed out emphatically, without raising his voice, "We are in a rock avalanche zone." I clearly saw it now.

He said, "There's been a slide recently," and cautioned me to be quiet, to step along, keep an eye and ear out, not to kick any rocks, and watch Rah-jud, the other guide 50 yards away. If he told me what to watch Rah-jud for, I missed it. I felt like an advancing base runner watching a third base coach in a baseball game. The problem was, if he gave a sign, I might not know what it meant. "Dear God, I need some help here."

Big and small boulders were all scattered about us, with the trail visible here and there, often covered by rocky debris of the slide. "Holy shit," excuse my French, I thought. I had to walk around slide remains in many spots. This 50 yard journey was memorable for the wrong reasons.

I followed instructions and prayed for myself and all of us. I breathed a little easier upon reaching Rahjud on the other side of the slide zone. My prayers were answered—"Runner safe on reaching third base." We all made it through fine.

Weeks before I left for Nepal, my lifetime friend Steve Owen mailed me a shirt from Disney World in sunny Florida which introduced a new ride that year called Forbidden Mountain. Named for Mount Everest, the new ride was said to be "bad" in the day's vernacular for thrills and fun. I had the shirt with me at the real Everest. I didn't like the name of the ride or the words on the T-shirt when first I saw it. Yet, the words now had me thinking.

I noticed the sun and clouds were doing quite a dance since we left Gorak Shep. Sometimes we had a quick glimpse of the Himalayan Mountain range's magnificence, but usually the clouds stayed low. We were high on a ridge now and far in the distance I could see the red, white, blue, yellow, and green colors of prayer flags strung in all directions. Next I made out the colors and contours of what must be expedition tents. "Base Camp is ahead," I told myself, although the distance seemed interminable. Still, I thought, "Praise the Lord and rock and roll. My physical eye now is on the prize itself!"

We plodded slowly along the ridge, with some uphill inclination but no real climbing now. And the trail was in pretty good shape.

So we moved along—my dream in sight. I noticed a headache, an attention-getter. I had more trouble drawing breath and realized it had been that way for a while. Another attention getter.

There was more to see of the frozen Khumbu Glacier on my right, and again I heard the loud creaking sounds of its movement. Again, the trail grew narrow and I watched my steps.

Now I viewed Everest winking from within the clouds. And there, clearly, was the Khumbu Icefall, its relief showing in detail. The Icefall was center stage within a semi-circle of three of the highest mountains on Earth. Oh, my God – I could see it. Lo, those many pictures in books later, my eyes saw the mountain, highlighted by Nuptse on the right, Lohtse in the center above the Icefall, and Everest itself on the left. I was close enough now to see individual tents at Base Camp.

Everest Base Camp is situated within a box canyon. That is to say the trail comes to a halt with some of the world's highest mountains serving as walls on several sides. The area is the size of a soccer field, maybe bigger. It is a somewhat level, but unstable, rocky moraine situated across from the Icefall. Big and small rocks of every shape are everywhere. Tents for sleeping, bigger dining and meeting tents, smaller toilet tents, and outdoor showers form this temporary camp that exists from March to May. They even have a satellite dish. Several Buddhist altars were constructed for prayers and "puja" ceremonies—to purify the climbers and offer blessings and prayers for safe climbing by monks who visit from Tengboche Monastery. Colorful prayer flag banners were strung from the altars where the wind would catch the colorful squares and lift their written prayers upward. Also, I saw the remains of a crashed helicopter.

We carried on for maybe 15 more minutes and then we arrived. Oh, my God—the mountains, the Icefall, the tents of Base Camp were around us. The Icefall was maybe two soccer fields away, and the foot of Everest right before us. Clouds shrouded the mountain from our view as though it was shy, not wishing to reveal more of itself right then. I was speechless, in absolute awe, standing beside my young friend Deckland, looking up at the mountain. And suddenly there came a sound like rolling thunder. My attention was drawn high up the mountain, where, out of the shroud came a descending white cloud of snow. The cloud picked up speed and rocketed along, growing in size and strength and speed.

"Avalanche! Oh, my God." I mouthed the words but don't think I found breath to voice them. I stared with vague awareness at what could be impending disaster. Deckland, next to me, swung into action taking pictures. Faintly I considered whether we were out of range, and it seemed we were. I gaped at the developing downward rampaging white tsunami engulfing everything in its path. It roared on and on, growing wider. An avalanche pushes high speed air before it full of powerful destructive force. This hits before the tons of snow and ice.

My clarity to act had been compromised by all the aforementioned signals. Typical responses for Walter Glover at this point should have included:

a) Say prayers that Deckland and I not be entombed by this mother, as it seemed to have us in its cross hairs, even if we were a long ways away;

b) Say prayers for safety for anyone else between Deckland and I and where the avalanche's storming cascade would take it;

c) Move from where we were; and,

d) Reach for a camera, as Deckland did, to take a picture.

I did none of these things. I simply stood motionless and mouthed, "Avalanche! Oh, my God." Again, failing to perform one or all of the tasks signaled that I was in distress and without clarity. Thankfully, the avalanche played out at the bottom of the mountain long before it reached us. The avalanche and my non-response screamed at me: "I am exhausted and running on fumes."

I slowly surmised that my present condition was not equal to the environment and forces at play. I felt humbled before this Holy Grail of a towering mountain. I was, however, moved into some action by the sight of the avalanche. I managed to collect slivers of rock son Andy had asked me to bring him from Base Camp. I knew I didn't need extra weight in my backpack, so the stones were small. Then, I snapped pictures, marveling in disbelief at the jumble of ice blocks the size of vehicles and even buildings making up the frozen river that is the Icefall. I tried to imagine what the Sherpas and climbers went through to navigate this, let alone how the Icefall Doctors fixed rope and put in ladders to get climbers up. I gaped at the shoulders of Everest—did I see the tiny figures of climbers?

I stood in awe and reverence of the mountain and its environment, its forces, and the Maker who created them. Here and there through the clouds, I glimpsed what the mountain would let me see of its bulk. The mountain, still shy, revealed itself for brief moments. Clouds came and went, then enveloped the entire mountain. It seemed my audience was over. Then, I curled up like a corkscrewing snail seeking shelter in its shell atop a rock and went to sleep near where the rest of our group had assembled.

I rested on the "porch" below the roof of the world. My head was now throbbing, and my weary legs had come along to keep my head company. I slept restlessly for perhaps 15 minutes. I must have seemed an ignoble sight to the majestic mountain—a tuckered-out buckeroo senior Hoosier from the cornfields of Indiana. Having given my all, I was in surrender.

Mike and son Ben arrived with pastry and cookies for everyone in our group. They had just visited "The World's Highest Bakery" and bought a bunch of goodies. I ate most of a pastry. The food helped. I drank some water. More help.

I asked Mike, "Did you used to go to the bakery and buy pastries and bring them home to your kids?"

Mike and son Ben looked at each other and laughed. "All the time," Mike said, marveling at my insight.

To myself, I thought: "I am mentally muddled here, but at least I can still think of my beloved Aunt Angie who used to buy bakery sweets for me when I was a child, and still continued doing this for other young children she loved—the Lees of Bedford—when she was in her late 80s."

I knew I was weak. I knew I had to retrace three to four hours of downhill walking to return to Gorak Shep where we would spend the night. I drank some water, but I still hadn't interpreted all the Danger Zone signs. Perhaps intuitively, I took an altitude prescription drug, Diamox, hoping it would help. Since arriving, I had taken Diamox every morning and sometimes at night. It helps the human body adjust to altitude. Taking it seemed like a good idea, but I was not thoughtfully and analytically looking in the rearview mirror of the last 18 hours, at how sloppily I performed and how poorly I reasoned. Thankfully, the pastry, the water, the Diamox, and the restless 15 minutes of sleep helped me.

As we begin our trek, going down in elevation, I start breathing richer, more oxygenated air. My legs were still going, but they felt knackered. I still had the throbbing headache, but it lessened as we descended. Then, remarkably, as more blood reached my brain in the richer oxygenated air, I finally began to connect the signs. Whoa! I missed three meals. I didn't sleep well last night, my first night on the trek not to. I was unsteady on my feet. I had a throbbing headache, plus my lack of reaction when the avalanche stormed down Everest. These were all signs of what had to be acute mountain sickness.

Then, suddenly I had a revelation—I remembered I had Dexamethasone, a rescue steroid that would goose my metabolism. Alas, it was in my other bag down the mountain at Gorak Shep. A bad word crossed my lips as I lashed into myself. However, we were going down. And the air kept getting thicker, little by little.

As is said and written about field and court athletes or marathoners running their course, playing their games—I left everything up there. I exhausted all my resources on the trek to Base Camp. And now I took one plodding step after another. But it was easier to breathe, and my headache eased some. Did I have a hunger pang, maybe? I was drinking water.

It was all I could do to descend to our frontier outpost at Gorak Shep. Finally, when we arrived there, I drank some hot chocolate, went to bed, and, thank God, took a Dexamethasone. Instantly I felt relief. At dinner I still wasn't hungry, but forced myself to eat because I knew my tank was empty of fuel. Likewise, I drank water and tea. Lots of water. I headed to bed early.

Deckland said Ingrid was okay, but just didn't have Base Camp within her. Thank God for her safety. Deckland, Ben and Mike, and Tom and Trina also made it to Base Camp. Along with me. Ingrid we would collect on the way back, as well as Ron and Eddie.

Funny, maybe it was just me, but I don't remember a lot of celebrating that night at dinner from any of us. To tell the truth, I remember little of dinner.

Before I turned in to bed, Dorzee asked me if tomorrow I wanted to climb up Kala Patar to its peak of 18,200 feet. I said simply, "Dorzee, thanks for asking. I don't have to answer that question right now do I?"

He responded, "No."

I said, "Let me get some sleep and let's talk about it again in the morning."

As I fell into bed, for the few minutes I was awake I sought God's will on climbing Kala Patar, something I'd hoped and planned to do. Given that day's developments and my performance, I felt uncertain. But for the night, I just let it go. I felt weaker than I had ever been. Depleted totally. Nonetheless, I made it to Mount Everest Base Camp. And back. Hallelujah. I would deal with Kala Patar tomorrow.

And I had a good, if not great night's sleep. I felt some restlessness, but slept 10 to 11 hours without even a visit to the loo. That wasn't a good sign, however. I still didn't have enough liquid in me to pee, despite my best efforts to hydrate.

Thursday, 10 May, 2007

I awakened at early light, rested but my body sore all over. I thought, "Even my hair and finger nails and toe nails are sore." And I laughed a little at this. Laughter was good sign. My favorite boxer was a hero of mine – Muhammed Ali. I saw him in many fights. I felt like I'd been in the ring getting pummeled by Ali. Another laugh.

But what about Kala Patar? Should I go, or not? No answer came. I went down some stairs to find the loo. Ouch. Stairs were tough going.

Coming out of the loo, there was Dorzee. "Walter good morning. Do you wish to go to Kala Patar today?"

"I'm thinking about it, Dorzee," I said.

"Well," he said, "Make up your mind because we are going to leave in 20 minutes." Now, I understood his haste.

This was a difficult decision. I truly wanted to go up and see the majestic panorama of the Himalayan Range. Kala Pata is high enough at 18,200 and far enough—a mile and or more away from

Everest and its neighbors—that you get an IMAX-like view of the highest peaks in the world, right before your eyes. I wanted to stand even higher than yesterday's 17,600 feet of elevation. Hmm, that sounded greedy, I thought. And I suddenly knew that going would be a mistake. All was not well with me yesterday, and returning to an altitude even higher than Base Camp a few hours later would be dumb.

I had only walked away from a few things in my life. I looked long and hard at Corbett's Couloir at Jackson Hole, Wyoming, before deciding it was beyond my skiing ability, which is pretty good, I've been told. I walked away from that in peace as I had walked away from a Bedford stone quarry high dive when I was younger. Although, with that quarry challenge unmet, I went back when I was at my 25th high school reunion and soared in a front layout swan dive from the same spot. Something about second opportunities, I suppose.

But for today, I decided yesterday had sucked all my reserves from me. Prudence was quietly dictating with firmness that I say, "No thank you," and peacefully walk away again, head up. Besides, I reasoned with good sense of re-born clarity, on return from Kala Patar to our camp, we still had a goodly day of trekking ahead of us. I thanked my Sherpa friend and declined. He smiled and nodded. As I walked back up those stairs from the loo to my room, the decision was confirmed as my legs ached on these simple wooden steps.

A passage in Exodus chapter 2 in the Old Testament concerns the name "Gershom," which translates to being an alien in a foreign land. A flatlander weakened by these mighty and high peaks, Gershom could be my name, I thought. I paired that with a verse from Psalm 18: "God enables me to stand on the heights." Though I wouldn't stand at 18,200 feet atop Kala Patar today, yesterday at age

59, I stood at 17,600 feet at Mount Everest Base Camp. Yesterday made me feel like both Gershom, and the subject of the Psalmist. And it made me laugh when I remembered the ancient Hebrew writers wrote of "mountains" near the Temple. Those mountains were only 5,000 feet high. What would those ancient writers have thought of the Himalayas?

As it turned out, only the youngsters made the Kala Patar climb. Ben was 22 and Deckland not much older. They were the only two of our group to climb it, accompanied by one of our young Sherpas. Good for the youth.

I felt weak and a little head achy at breakfast but that didn't disrupt my appetite. I knew I needed to eat, and now I even wanted to eat—I was famished. I gobbled up eggs and pancakes and drank the fresh, more or less, coffee. At least the coffee was brewed from real beans. The three eggs were somewhere between over easy and scrambled. But I learned early in the expedition trek to let go of any preferences on how food looked, tasted, or was presented. And these eggs and pancakes had an okay taste. And I drank lots of H2o.

Mike and I saw each other outside the lodge, under the most brilliant azure bluebird sky I had ever seen. I wondered again what the thin air did to colors at this elevation. And there stood Everest in all its glory. Not a cloud in the sky. "If the view here is this good, what our young men should see from Kala Pathar must be stupendous," I said to Mike, who agreed happily, knowing his son Ben was probably up there by this time.

I ask Mike to take a pic of me in the foreground with Everest over my shoulder. My blue top picked up some of the sky color and my gray hair matched the mountain top. I sported a pair of children's sunglasses with blue frames formed to look like sun bursts. St. Vincent Jennings Hospital gave the glasses away at the county 4H Fair. I wore them from time to time on the trail and they would always generate smiles. My accompanying line was: "We Everest trekkers cannot take ourselves too seriously." All these years later, this remains one of my favorite pics from the trek. Thanks again, Mike for a great shot.

Deckland and Ben returned with great stories of their views from their climb to 18,200. Wistfully, I wished I'd been with them. Yet I was happy for them and knew I made the right decision.

We would head to Pheriche on this day, a hike of about 2.5 hours, descending a couple of thousand feet and walking six or seven miles. I remembered reading it had a hospital or medical clinic run by an international group of volunteer medical doctors.

We returned through the cemetery, where Mike recalled the Jewish memorial and had Ben take a photo of him putting a stone on that memorial. Adding stones atop cairns or mani religious stones is a Sherpa and Nepalese custom. I asked Mike if I might make a suggestion, to email his picture if he found an email address for the family. He liked the idea.

At this point, I was missing my family, wondering what my sons were up to. I also wondered about my hospital, St. Vincent Jennings in North Vernon. Joseph Roche, my CEO there, met with me right before I left and said I should treat the expedition as a kind of pilgrimage. In that spirit he said, "Don't be thinking about us here. We'll be fine. Take it all in."

As soon as we arrived at Pheriche, one of our number checked into the medical clinic. He had suffered from difficulty breathing since Base Camp, plus nausea and fatigue. His recreational pursuit was marathon open water swimmer, including in the ocean. He was strong and fit, with great lung capacity. And yet the doctor, an American, diagnosed him with acute mountain sickness and put him on oxygen for two hours.

I visited with the man around the fire in the common room for a bit. We were still high and the air remained "thin." As he described his symptoms, I thought, "That's me!" But I felt much better and didn't feel the need for a consult. The Diamox and the Dexamethasone helped—and I believe I was the only one in the crew who carried those elevation drugs. I was grateful for Dr. Jones, back in Indiana.

Having said that, I still took a nap after we arrived and I rested comfortably. My appetite, after being good at breakfast, fell off again that evening. I knew we'd be on the trail for nearly seven hours the next day, trekking all the way to Namche. We had recollected Ingrid who seemed fine, and we were seven again. We would soon reunite with Ron and Eddie at Namche and return to our full strength of nine.

Ingrid was glad to see us—especially Deckland of course. She was sweet, kind and pleasant to be around. She told me her father back in Australia was a volunteer for the St. Vincent de Paul Society, an international Vincentian social justice outreach of the Catholic Church to help those in poverty. Vincent, the founder of the international health ministry with which I am associated, was a stalwart advocate for the poor. But who was this? A young woman who seemed familiar showed up at our teahouse. She was the woman I first met at the airport back in Kathmandu. She went, not to Everest Base Camp, but trekked to some lakes in the Everest region. She was staying in the next town a few miles over.

"I came over the mountain to see Ben," she said. Mike, Ben's dad, had introduced the two young people when Rebekkah, the young woman, and Mike and I drove into the Shangri-La Hotel parking lot in Kathmandu. However, the intended reunion of Ben and Rebekkah, which they arranged back in Kathmandu when they looked at their expedition routes and schedules, had a twist.

Ben heard she was in the next town and went over there to meet her, while she came to meet him. Taking different routes, they didn't intersect. Dorzee stepped in to help and arranged for one of the young Sherpas to escort her to Ben.

I heard later that within a few hours they did successfully have a reunion, thanks to Dorzee. When we returned to the Shangi-La Hotel a week later, I teased Mike saying, "Invite me to the wedding." Mike was a lawyer, Ben was headed to Yale Law, and Rebekkah was already at Stanford Law.

Friday, 11 May, 2007

I slept fairly well. I read and prayed over Isaiah's verses on walking, for this day. Isaiah chapter 40 verse 31: "They that hope in the Lord will renew their strength. They will soar as with eagles' wings; they will run and not grow weary; walk and not grow faint." The parts about "not grow weary ... not grow faint" constituted my prayer. I prayed it for me. I prayed it for all of us. We would spend seven hours going up and down—mostly down. Thank You. Destination, Namche.

The Khumbu cough, as it is called, is a mostly dry, non-productive cough—a common symptom of being high in the mountains. It is annoying to do and can be irritating to hear. For the past few days we had all become a choir of Khumbu coughers. Theologically, I worked my brain around applying Isaiah to our coughing. "Cough and not grow faint," is what I got; a stretch in reasoning I suppose. Oh well, I tried thinking of the Khumbu coughing as scriptural music ... or rock and roll... No melodic tie there; too much of a stretch.

We continued mostly going downhill, although we also faced some steep uphill sections as we headed back to Namche Bazaar, the trail's capital. And today was a long, wet, ordeal. "Slog" would be an apt description. We were seven hours away, and it seemed we spent 75 percent of the day in a downpour. The final stretch was a Hoosier "toad strangler" and I felt wet everywhere; cold too.

If my calculations and written notes are correct for the last three days, including that day, we had truly been on the move.

We trekked 9 hours (more?) to reach Base Camp and return to Gorak Shep;

The next day we trekked 4.5 hours; and

This day would be 6.5 hours.

When I did the calculations, my tired legs ached even more when I saw on paper what we'd been up (and down) to. We performed 20 (more?) hours of trekking in three days, for an average of about seven hours a day. All this at 16 to 17,000 feet of altitude, going both up and down. We each carried a fair bit of fatigue, plus some illness, plus our backbacks. What did they weight—20 pounds each, methinks. Come on Isaiah ! "Walk – Trek – and not grow faint."

When we reached Namche I knew a shower and rest were in my immediate future. And then we would be graced with an off day. Thank you God—You rested on Sunday, right? Well our rest would be on Saturday, but this day of rest came none too soon. For our Jewish brothers and sisters, Saturday is the Sabbath—that worked for me.

The route to Namche was slick and slippery. A steady rain fell, often heavy. During much of the day we were totally socked in, as though we walked within the clouds from which the rains fell.

We did receive a colorful and scented surprise in Namche: Spring had arrived during the few days we were gone. Huge rhododendron bushes were blooming, looking more like trees than the bushes I knew at home. They formed a canopy over the trail in many spots, their blooms a beautiful contrast to the mud of the trail and the little vegetation we'd recently seen. The colors above at Base Camp were mostly shades of white and gray. There were elements of rock and air, and our moisture was ice and snow. Well, this day's moisture was rain, and plenty of it. But the natural garden also included delicate crocus here and there, wild volunteer flowers dotting the landscape. All their colors dripped raindrops, a sure sign of spring.

We encountered long upward treks over hills, and I especially remembered one steep hill we had walked down while heading outbound to Base Camp. Now, it was uphill. For this challenging stretch I took a lesson from riding my bicycle named Trigger. Sailah called our group to a rest stop midway up the hill, but I learned that breaking my momentum while bicycling up a hill made the rest of that climb even tougher. Applying that to trekking, I learned breaks in the middle of a hill didn't necessarily help. So on this long uphill, I simply said, "I'm going to keep going and you catch me at the top. I'll wait there."

Good naturedly, Sailah called, "We'll see you in Namche!" It worked. I had strong legs going all the way up. However, I drew a frown or two from a couple of our group when they reached me at the top. Did they think I was showing off? "Whatever" I told myself.

At the top I also ran into a guy with a Boston Red Sox cap and we had a delightful chat while I waited. We continued talking as my group walked past. I caught up with them and on we went—our steps as unrelenting as the rain.

At lunch I ate drinks of soup and bites of rice. I still hadn't fully regained my appetite. I was afraid to eat, and afraid not to. It felt as though I would vomit if I ate a full serving of food, yet if I didn't eat enough I wouldn't have sufficient strength for the journey. So I faced a Catch 22 with my appetite.

As we made our long descent into Namche, I began feeling better. My Khumbu cough subsided with the oxygen-rich air and, as it became easier to breathe, my headache mostly disappeared. Now perhaps I would rediscover my appetite. I sloshed as I walked, with rainwater inside my boots. I was wet inside and out. Finally, Namche Bazaar came into view below us. Yeah!

Our reward as we approached was harder rainfall. Despite being soaked, I felt warm but not overheated. "Thank you God and my yellow-black Columbia jacket and its makers. Thank you for being my maker and giver of body, mind, and spirit." The Isaiah prayer was paying dividends.

Ron and Eddie were already at our Namche teahouse, having come down earlier from Tengboche Monastery where last we saw them. We had a nice reunion, but only two things were on my mind: Exit the wet clothes and step into a hot shower.

This would be the first time I bathed my entire body in 13 days— probably a personal record going back to birth. This was also my third weekend away from my family and my home. Lord, did I miss my family, and my home. The shower's hot water provided some solace – even though it mixed with a few tears.

My soaked clothes and my grimy outer clothes went to the laundry service our lodge offered. Another blessing. I began reflecting on how this month might change my life, but the musing was short-lived because dinnertime arrived—and a celebratory feast for dinner awaited us Namche Bazaar style.

We had yak steak dinner with all the trimmings. I sat near the fire with Deckland and Ingrid, who had just arrived at Namche. The trek was slow going for them because Ingrid's gait had slowed and she was struggling.

Ron and Eddie were present for the first meal time since we separated and it was nice to see them. They laughed a lot. Ingrid, Deckland, and I compared notes about how far we'd come. They, like me, were subdued. Fatigue had taken its toll. Our team member who was ill and treated at Periche was absent, still sick. Thankfully, my appetite was partly restored and the yak meat was moist and tender.

I drank an Everest beer that tasted divine. Then I drank a second one, slowly, reflectively, in part because I found it semi-frozen. I didn't care. I ate fairly well and my food stayed put. I felt quietly content.

Feeling flat out exhausted, before long I began thinking about the white sheets on my twin bed.

As I left the room Ron and Eddie sang the old Roy Rogers' song, "Happy Trails to you." The words made for a nice sentiment. Despite that, I noticed distance developing between myself and some members of the group and me. I didn't understand this and wondered what I did, or didn't do. I was sensitive enough to be concerned, but well-integrated enough to not let it steal my peace. And I was much too tired to think any more about it.

Saturday, 12 May, 2007

I slept around the clock—almost 12 hours of sound sleep. Now I had phlegm in the remnants of my Khumbu cough. Hopefully, that meant it was nearly done.

Through the walls I heard Aussie tones from next door. I didn't eavesdrop, but the muted conversation reminded me of my family big-time, my friends, my home. Despite what my boss said about not thinking about the hospital, I also missed the people there. As a pastoral counselor, I had intimate talks with many of them and we formed bonds of friendship. I felt genuinely alone and even lonely, but the cure would be simple: Returning home.

However, on that morning I was still around the world, 15,000 miles from home. Walls had gone up within the group that exacerbated my loneliness. I've always been blessed in knowing how to make friends and keep them. I can honestly say I have many friends, new and old. Since leaving on the trek I had befriended people in our group and been befriended, but it appeared some of them were de-friending me, as they say on Facebook. No use confronting them; people are entitled to their opinions. But their attitudes made me long for home and intimacy that much more.

Today was the Saturday marketplace, a big stage for mostly small vendors to play on. Many, many customers climbed up, down, and across Kumbu hill country to reach Namche and peruse the stalls and stands. Sales seemed to be brisk—rupees were changing hands, especially among the many trekker types who'd come to the market. Having already contributed to the economy of Nachme, I didn't find anything to buy at the bazaar, but I did purchase more gifts from the village shops.

I remembered that, back home, this was commencement day at St. Meinrad, my seminary. Having graduated only a year ago, I knew some of the new graduates. I smiled to myself, recalling how I told Kyle, my academic advisor, that I planned to ride my bicycle Trigger across the stage to collect my diploma. I always had Trigger with me on campus to ride during week end classes. I rode before class, at lunchtime, and sometimes after classes ended for the day, so people often saw me on the bike. Evidently Kyle wasn't sure about my true intentions, because he and one of the leadership priests visited the pre-ceremony lunch to emphasize the importance of *walking* across the stage.

Back at the bazaar, I continued enjoying the day of rest. No rain and plenty of relaxation, mostly by myself. After visiting the shops, I sat in front of some places to let the sun touch my face as though I were on a beach. I listened to music from a guitar passed among three or four men who took turns playing, and sometimes singing. This week, a number of young monks had walked down from Tangboche Monastery to shop and visit. They kept to themselves, seeming to travel in pairs, and avoided eye contact with people they didn't know.

Seeing their reticence made me glad I visited a monk on his home court at the monastery. I also reflected on how blessed I was in 1999 to be in the presence of the Dalai Lama when he led an Inter-faith Prayer Vigil at St. Charles Church in Bloomington. I attended with my friend Tom Hill from Columbus, who later became a deacon in the Catholic Church. Tom and I, along with about 800 other people, enjoyed a remarkable spiritual event.

My shopping and relaxation day ended in the lodge where we viewed the IMAX video of the 1996 tragedy on Everest, the heroic rescue work by the IMAX team, and their successful ascent of the mountain. We especially enjoyed the segment about the trek to Everest Base Camp, since we'd just returned from there. Afterward I played a card game with Deckland and Ingrid, then off to bed.

I was ready to be home.

Sunday, 13 May, 2007

This day featured a leisurely four hour trek to Phakding, nearly all downhill, especially the big descent at the outskirts of Namche. We trekked through what is called the Blue Pine Forest. We enjoyed the warm spring temperature with a light breeze. The path was easy walking, except for a little mud here and there from the big downpour a few days earlier.

I felt stronger—I had my legs back and could stride strongly as I did before the acute mountain sickness. The headache and cough? Gone! The bridge that so terrified me because it spanned 100 feet above the gorge was now like a walk in the park. I strode confidently across it with my thumbs tucked inside my pack's waist belt – no need to even hold onto the wire rails. Other than my yearning for home, this was a fine day to be on the trail.

Farmers were planting crops in the nearby fields, most likely barley, potatoes, and rice. I laughed, remembering one of the tea house restaurants that featured 14 different kinds of rice or potato dishes. Fortunately I was done with those foods for a while. And our wonderful Sherpas always brought us tea or powdered coffee in the morning. It would be weeks before I let those items cross these lips again.

We reached Phakding after four hours of trekking. One more trek day—tomorrow we would reach Lukla. I decided to celebrate this beautiful day by drinking an Everest beer with lunch. We were outside, so I choose a spot to get some sun on my face. This interlude reminded me of being an undergrad at IU on a weekend at Brown County State Park, in Nashville, on a spring day.

During this day I spent time getting to know the younger Sherpas. From the shirt he was wearing, I discovered Ramish had interests beyond the mountain trail—he had run a marathon through the mountains, from Namche to Lukla. I offered a trade of one of the printed T-shirts I had, but I doubt there was enough salt in Tibet, or woolen goods from Nepalese yaks, or gold at Fort Knox to convince Ramish to part with his marathon shirt. I couldn't imagine running up and down at that altitude, let alone covering 26 miles of rugged terrain. Ramish was unbelievably strong and utterly humble.

I once ran a marathon distance, but every slow step of that five hours was on flat ground. Running a marathon in the mountains was an unbelievable performance by the athlete Ramish.

And we soon discovered another hidden talent—Ramish was also an artist who did oil painting. He invited us to his studio and revealed stunning paintings. They were for sale and I settled on a beautiful oil rendition of the pyramidic mountain of Ama Dablam with Tengboche Monatery in the foreground—a striking view of both. For me, this work of art portrayed the majesty of God at work in nature, and man at work in God. I happily paid the asking price without the customary negotiating.

Rahjud and Ramish let me help prepare dinner that night. Raw potatoes were placed in a small, barrel like wooden container and mashed using a sturdy limb broken from a tree. They showed me how to thrust the limb downward through a hole in the top of the container. We all laughed about my clumsiness in learning.

That night Rahjud was with his wife and brother, pursuing family time and one of his hobbies—playing pool. Phakding had a pool hall that consisted of a large room with one table. The brothers teased one another as they played, and the wife teased them all by scattering the balls and laughing. Music wafted from a boom box. I was more than ready to hear "Back Home Again in Indiana."

My time with the young Sherpas reminded me I needed to organize the gifts I brought for them, in addition to the cash tips I planned to pay. Tomorrow we'd reach Lukla and soon be parting company.

While preparing for bed I received a huge gift. As I lay in the darkness of my room in the tea house, from the window I could see luminous stars vividly sparkling in the night sky. And—look at that! A shooting star raced past my window. I whispered, "God, you made the heavens and the Earth and all that are in them. You count the stars and call them all by name." I remembered the verse from Psalms, or was it Isaiah in the Old Testament?

The stars were a gift for my eyes and for my ears came another gift—the steady throb of a nearby creek, a steady, pleasant, meditative pulse of moving water. Not the music of the pool hall, or "Back Home Again in Indiana," but it gently lulled me to sleep. This reminded me of a springtime at Vail Colorado, when I opened a window to hear a creek streaming across a rocky bed nearby. Happy sounds for me that infuse calmness.

Monday, 14 May, 2007

At sunrise I awakened to more sounds, but not the pleasant creek. Helicopters were flying low overhead in the direction of Phakding. It seemed they were following our trek route through the valley toward Namche. I wondered if this was a rescue effort. Was help needed urgently at Base Camp.? I prayed for the people

I had met who were on the mountain, like Johan, Martin, and the IMAX crew.

Soon the choppers moved out of earshot, letting the gurgling creek and twittering birds reclaim the air space. The invasive sound of the choppers reminded me that we'd heard no vehicular internal combustion or diesel engines since beginning the trek. Well, perhaps a generator here and there, and small motors to move water. How refreshing!

Today would be our final trek—four hours of walking to Lukla from where we started on 30 April. This day was 14 May, two weeks plus.

My strongest memory of the final trek to Lukla was seeing outbound people heading upward to Base Camp. They looked fresh and fit, and their clothes were clean. They jabbered and pointed like many people in our group did at the beginning, although everyone in our group was now more subdued. For the outbound rookies this would be day one of their trek, and they were experiencing their first few hours. For them I prayed, "May it go well for you. Learn as much about yourself as you do the mountain and its environment." And for myself, I prayed in gratitude for my learnings during these 15 days trekking to and from Mount Everest Base Camp.

Dorzee said we racked up nearly 100 miles with our side trips and acclimatizing miles. "That doesn't count trips to the loo," he added, laughing.

When I recalculated this at home I came up with 85 miles estimated—sans the loos. I liked Dorzee's version better, and he surely knew more than me. Said another way: The total distance I trekked up and down, and up and down in Nepal equals the distance from Columbus north, beyond St. Vincent Indianapolis Hospital, to Carmel, and on into Westfield's Cool Creek Park; or, from Columbus, to Bloomington, and back to Columbus. However, in Nepal the elevation was 8,500 feet up to 17,600 feet. The highest point in Brown county is about 1,000 feet, and in Columbus and Bartholomew county the elevation is close to 630 feet.

Before leaving Nepal, I thought about the things I learned:

- The time trekking and climbing in the Himalaya was equal parts adventure, risk, wellness, exhilaration, exhaustion and spirituality. And homesickness.

- The importance of a guide to a safe and successful experience in mountain terrain and an extreme environment is vital. Don't dare leave home or your lodge without your guide.

- The compatibility of the group in which you are a member enhances the journey. I advise going with someone you know and trust, who is at least your equal in fitness.

- While the destination is the end attraction, the journey is most important. You should learn as much, and perhaps more, about yourself, than the region you visit.

- Mindfulness, attentiveness, and openness will increase the mountain's ability to teach you.

- Where I come from and communities at home and in the West take so many things for granted, beginning with fresh water and sanitary conditions;

- And, "Fear not" are words found throughout the Old and New Testaments of the Bible and in other sacred writings. Joshua is told four times in the opening verses of the book that bears his name to "be courageous." Risk-taking and adventure prompt one to take inventory of feelings that surround courage and fearlessness. I received an abundance of learning in this area. Everest Base Camp was some introduction, that's for certain.

We arrived from where we started, Lukla, at 10:30 a.m. "Home again, home again," I told myself, although I surely knew this

Nepalese village was nowhere near my home near Donner Park in Columbus, Bartholomew County, Indiana, USA. I would have to find my way there from this way station halfway around the world. This would be true of too many days in the busy metro area of Kathmandu.

From home, I had packed T-shirts and other clothing for the Sherpas and porters which I distributed to happy receivers. I also contributed to the community kitty Dorzee arranged for us. Financial tips are the customary way to show gratitude on the mountain, but the crew seemed surprised and pleased with the articles of clothing I gave them.

I gathered my prescription drugs and other toiletries for the little hospital in the village, and our team members contributed a few more items. I walked about a mile to the hospital. The pharmacist, who spoke English, gratefully accepted the meds and toiletries. He also invited me to tour the hospital and took great pride in showing me around the small, but immaculate, facility. He introduced me to a couple of physicians who didn't speak English. The entire hospital contained limited equipment, several examination rooms, and a few overnight rooms.

The pharmacist told me their patients came from nearby villages, and also included trekkers and climbers. They called this a hospital, but by Western standards it seemed more like a clinic. Some of the patients walked days to get here—no 9-1-1 service here. In the West, we take so many things for granted, I reminded myself. If we see an accident or someone in distress, we simply pull out a cell phone, call for help, and wait for a trained medical crew with equipment and transportation to arrive. Even in a small town, the trip to a hospital is short and excellent medical care is always available. The contrast was great.

The hospital staff appreciated the items I gave them on behalf of our group, and I felt a warm glow about making the extra effort to donate our leftover supplies. The tour, in turn, gave me a greater appreciation of the medical resources we have at home.

Now came the time the crew waited for—payday as the expedition officially ended. Dorzee called our group together for the customary counting out of the money the crew would be paid, plus our tips. Dorzee handled this himself in full view of his crew and us. We were present as a kind of accountability and appreciation step that traced to mountaineering's beginnings when the British began climbing here in the 1920s. I understood from my readings about the accountability piece and I knew we are supposed to watch. I pointed this out to some neighbors in the room, but they watched only for a moment and returned to playing cards. The process did seem to take forever, so I begin playing cards too. The crew, on the other hand, watched the distribution with great interest. After all, this was their payday. Dorzee announced when the last porter received his pay, and he encouraged a round of applause which was roundly given. Then we could take photos of the crew.

Back in my room, I enjoyed my second shower on the expedition. The bathroom mirror startled me—my face and body were so thin.

I had dinner with Deckland and Ingrid, with whom I spent part of the afternoon trading digital pictures. They remained friendly from the first time I met them. As I write this six years after the trek, I've heard from them twice by email in the last year.

I fell into bed by 8 p.m. and slept like a little boy again—Thank you, God.

Tuesday, 15 May, 2007

Our final morning in the Himalayas had a brisk pace.

We ate a hurried breakfast at an early hour and it turned out our flight would be one of the first departing to Kathmandu. A large scale stood near the counter at the check-in point, so I removed my trek boots (the only pair of shoes I had with me at Everest) and stepped onto it. The meter read 167 pounds. I smiled, thinking, "I was on the see (not sea) food diet." I weighed exactly the same as when I left Columbus. The day before, looking at myself in the mirror, I thought I'd had lost weight. But my waistband still fitted snugly and comfortably. Even with the AMS and the loss of appetite, I must have gained back every pound, but it repositioned itself on my body—the mirror said so!

As other groups gathered at the airport I heard some Khumbu coughs among the incessant chattering of human voices. Then, the ignition of airplane motors and the turning of blades. Noise flooded into my world.

In what seemed only minutes we boarded, buckled in, and the plane was tearing over the downhill runway to gain speed and get lift before it fell off the edge of the mountain. Remembering how we bounced in on our approach, I was praying and praying and praying. "Let this be safe and smooth." We did safely lift off and sailed away into air space.

I had already said my farewell to Everest, plus a generous thank you. And to God I gave thanks and glory for His created order, and my body, mind, and spirit. Thanks too for safety. I always hope a trip will exceed my expectations, and that when I return home I am changed—for the better. Mount Everest Base Camp was a blessing on all counts.

Thirty minutes later we arrived at Kathmandu. Not long after that we reached the Shangri-La Hotel and I was at the pool reading *Uncomfortable with Uncertainty"* Pema Chodron's Buddhist classic. I rested and relaxed my weary bones.

In my room I gazed from my second floor window and noticed razor wire topping the compound wall just outside. Monkeys walked slowly through it to climb a tree and reach its fruit. I watched a monkey and a bird bicker over the rights to tree fruit.

Tomorrow would be one month away from home. Could that be right? I met for lunch with Deckland and Ingrid, and Ron and Eddie. All our conversation focused on heading home.

Wednesday, 16 May, 2007

This would be our final day at the Shangri-La in Kathmandu. I now felt way over this extended trip. When we flew from Lukla to Kathmandu I wished the plane was lifting off from Kathmandu, to Bangkok, to the USA.

I was invited to join the others at a Farewellin Dinner. My heart wasn't in this, but I went anyway. Some people were friendly, but others were not. What did boost my spirits, in addition to the friendliness of a few, was that the grounds of the hotel had been converted to a wedding wonderland. We learned that 400 guests were under the huge tent, in the big garden next to our dining area, having the time of their lives. I enjoyed watching them. Later, as my room's windows overlooked the gardens turned wonderland, I watched for a while and then just listened as the reception held sway until 2 a.m.

Thursday, 17 May, 2007

Finally, we flew out of Kathmandu. Another long day would pass before I deplaned in Indianapolis and walked into the arms of my younger son Andy. Eight more weeks would pass before I was at near one hundred percent physical capacity again, having endured acute mountain sickness and possibly the beginnings of cerebral edema. While I would ski the next winter, at first I didn't see myself climbing another mountain. Two years would pass before I returned to the world's big mountains with an expedition to Mount Kilimanjaro in Tanzania, Africa. You see, the voice started speaking to me again. And as a print interviewer years later would write, "This time I didn't argue with the voice."

Thanks to you God for the Everest adventure, for my safety, and for my wellness. Thank you for my reunion with family, friends, and those at the hospital. Thank you for my newfound appetite for mountains without ski lifts, amazing adventures, new cultures, and the treasures they all hold despite the dangers. Bless those with whom I shared the mountain. If I offended anyone, forgive me; and, let me forgive others. Let me integrate Mount Everest as experience into my life and let it speak, through me, to others.

Boudhanath Temple, Kathmandu, Nepal.

With Deckland and Ingrid, mates from Australia.

Walter and sirdar Dorzee at lower left with expedition crew.
Mount Everest in view above the clouds.

Having fun with beautiful carvings at the entry to
the revered Tengboche Monastery.

Tengboche Monastery.

Monastery portal or gate.

Sign indicating one of the many schools built by Sir Ed Hillary.

Mountain village.

*Wally visiting with a boy on route to
Everest Base Camp.*

Walter trekking behind guide Sailah to Everest Base Camp.

Taking a moment to reflect along the trail to Everest Base Camp.

Everest Base Camp at the foot of the Khumbu Icefall.

Avalanche rocketing down Mount Everest, crossing the Khumbu Icefall.

*Walter with guide and oil painter Ramish and his
rendering of Amadablan and Tengboche Monastery
(now hanging in Walter's home).*

SECTION 2: Mount Kilimanjaro

2. Mount Kilimanjaro

Kilimanjaro may be the best known mountain in the world, shadowed only by Everest. This mountain features stunning beauty, glaciers, a volcanic crater, and a sample of every climate zone on earth despite its location at the equator. In addition, Kilimanjaro is ancestral home to the human race.

My good friend David Ketchum from Columbus invited me to climb this mountain and I accepted the invitation to accompany him to Africa to see his mission field in Ghana and then climb Kilimanjaro in the Rift Valley of East Africa in Tanzania. How could I say no? Dave's gracious invite came while I was preparing for Everest. Glibly, I, who knew so little about mountains, said: "Put me in coach, give me the ball. Sure, I'll go. Thanks for inviting me."

Months later, feeling sick and exhausted after my return from Everest, I told him, "Davey, forget Kilimanjaro and that mountain stuff. For me it's one and done."

Eight weeks passed before my normal health returned after suffering acute mountain sickness and the possible beginnings of cerebral edema on the trek to Everest Base Camp.

My son Andrew had picked me up at Indianapolis International after my near-month long stay in Nepal. On greeting me at the airport and on the way home, seeing and hearing how I felt, Andy said, "Dad, you might have picked up a parasite. Go see the doctor."

Andy later told me I agreed to see the doctor, but I have no memory of that promise. A week later, when I was no better, he asked, "Well, what'd the doctor say?"

My "Huh?" did not impress Andy—a school teacher and soccer coach who made Dad feel like a delinquent pupil. In my jet-lagged, energy-depleted state, I spaced out his wise recommendation. After our second conversation I promptly reported to the principal, I mean the physician. The next week all my blood work came back clear.

I also contacted Dr. Jones, my travel and mountain physician specialist. As we talked through my condition, he said under-hydrating probably led to my problems—and that's when I was officially diagnosed with acute mountain sickness and a possible brush with cerebral edema. He expected I'd soon return to normal. "Just take it slow," he cautioned.

At this point I struggled to play tennis for 30 minutes, while before the trip I could play competitively for hours. A couple of months would pass before my energy level returned to 100 per cent and I could play tennis for a couple of hours at a stretch.

Several groups in Columbus asked me to give a presentation about my trek to Everest, so I developed a talk called Capacity to Dream. Audience members told me the presentation was "inspiring" and "a great story." Giving the talk energized me. As I began to physically feel better and reflect on the trip in public gatherings, I reconsidered my decision to abandon Kilimanjaro and Africa. While preparing for one of the public appearances, I asked myself, "If you're going to get up in front of people and talk about going to Everest, why aren't you considering Kilimanjaro?" I worked this through in my head.

Emotionally and mentally, I moved deliberately in my consideration of Kilimanjaro, taking a fair bit of time to sort through the complexities of planning another international mountaineering trip. I had moving parts to consider: The expense, being away from family again, physical training, and all the other preparations, such as choosing a guiding company and making travel arrangements.

Nevertheless, I called Dave and happily informed him of my change of heart.

As it turned out, Dave couldn't swing the trip. In my head, however, I had already committed.

And now I had a sound and benevolent idea I wanted to tie-in with the expedition. In the past I was blessed to write checks for the fundraising efforts of local projects, including bike rides, walks, runs, dance marathons, and other physical activities that raised money for good causes. As the leadership person for the St. Vincent Jennings Hospital Foundation, I told myself, "I could raise money for our hospital ministry." My only question was: "For which worthy project?" There were so many!

Early into my incubation of this idea, three circumstances that occurred independently of one another gave me a good idea.

I wanted to bring together our Foundation's board of directors with other Jennings county community leaders for two purposes: First, to invite their counsel and consensus on possible items the Foundation should consider funding. And second, I wanted community leaders who weren't familiar with St. Vincent Hospital, which was still new to the North Vernon and the Jennings county community, to know us better. Hopefully, both purposes would serve the Foundation's mission of helping the community better understand the hospital, which in turn would lead to greater support of the hospital and our Foundation. The meeting's timing coincided with my fundraising idea.

Our joint meeting had a wonderful turnout, with great ideas generated. The new people in the room appreciated the opportunity to visit the hospital, learn about us, and brainstorm ideas. And Foundation board members had many suggestions on priorities to fund, as did our visitors. One idea grabbed my attention right away: youth obesity problems. Our guests pointed out that Jennings County needed to help their many, many overweight kids.

The second circumstance, independent of the Foundation meeting, came from what St. Vincent Indianapolis called their Community Needs Assessment. This was done every other summer in each of the nearly 20 communities where St. Vincent had a hospital ministry. As we were so new, this would be the first assessment for Jennings County. Overseen by St. Vincent Hospital Indianapolis in conjunction with a Ph.D. program at Indiana University, we polled Jennings county residents to what people believed was needed in their personal lives and within the community. Results from the tabulation and scoring process came in around the time of the Foundation meeting. Youth obesity received a high score as an unmet need within the community. Hmmm.

Acting on this information, I sought out our pediatric medical staff. Sitting down with our lead physician, pediatric nurse practitioner and Linda Hefner and Lynne Henry, I asked them: "If I were able to raise funds through the Foundation for a medical issue in pediatrics, what would you have me raise money for?"

Lynne, who was chosen as Indiana's top nurse practitioner one year, looked at me, then glanced at Dr. Hefner, who was starting her practice after completing a pediatric residency at the University of Cincinnati, one of the top five pediatric schools in the United States. Lynne said, "Duhhh, Wally. Have you seen our patients? Have you seen the kids in this community? Go raise money for youth obesity."

Dr. Hefner nodded her agreement.

Well, alrighty then.

Now I had three confirmations that starting a prevention and treatment program for overweight children was a worthy project for St. Vincent Jennings. Mind you, I took no pre-conceived notions into this process, other than calling that first meeting. And I had no favorite for what the cause might be. All three of the confirmations were independent of each other. To me, it seemed the Holy Spirit was at work in the process. And the Spirit, Galun Lati in Cherokee, was speedy, too. All of this unfolded within two short weeks.

My next stop was to see Joseph Roche, my CEO at Jennings, and convey this information. It was autumn, 2008. I said, "Joe, next summer I'm going to follow up my Everest trip by climbing Mount Kilimanjaro in Tanzania, Africa. I can use the expedition to raise money for youth obesity here at our ministry. What do you think?"

Joe thought this was an excellent and creative idea. He was succinct: "Count on my support. Bring it up through the Foundation Board and I believe you'll be well supported."

At our next meeting, the Foundation Board enthusiastically endorsed the initiative of a mountain climb to raise money. No one else within St. Vincent, at Indianapolis or our many other hospitals large and small, had used mountain climbing to raise money; in general, we Hoosiers didn't do mountains.

This is the story of that expedition, its success, and its challenges, both in the mountains and with fundraising and other issues at the hospital. It is also the story of how the second climb became the gateway to my quest of the Seven Summits—and a story of success and challenges that led to raising $22,000 for St. Vincent Jennings to inaugurate their youth obesity prevention and treatment program.

Privately, I thought my fundraising would honor my Aunt Angie Meno, who was heavy as a child but later shed the pounds. "Aunt" as I called this passionate and fearless woman, was decades ahead of her time. She ate healthy with every meal and exercised daily—and I do mean daily, vigilantly into her ninth decade, even while a hospice patient. Her Catholic Christian faith and Italian roots sustained her through many a crisis and were the basis of her hope—"spronza" in Italian. Daily, she claimed her hope and her joy. She was my Godmother; a woman ahead of her time who understood and lived with the importance of "Body, Mind and Spirit" before I was born, before I knew those words were the foundation of Vincentian (St. Vincent) health care. She was an advocate for healthy living in the 1950s, before wellness became a buzz word or popular practice.

Tuesday, 9 June, 2009

At 0600 military time (6 a.m.), my son Dominic and I walked out the door with my luggage for the expedition to Tanzania, East Africa, destination Mount Kilimanjaro. My weight that morning was 166 pounds, a little above my high school weight and one pound under my current training weight. Who knew how much my luggage would weigh? I did know that my training backpack for this trip weighed 25 pounds, the weight I would carry on Kili. I had trekked every day with the pack while wearing my trek boots. I made certain that, of the three or more miles I walked every day, at least one mile was vertical—going up and down, up and down. Sometimes the up-down consisted of indoor or outdoor stairs. I used any vertical space I could find to help me train in Indiana for a mountain in Africa. And I wore the pack every day, plus the trek boots I would wear for the journey.

My prayer on the morning of departure was one of gratitude: "Thank you Creator God, Son Jesus, your Spirit. All I have, all I am, comes from you."

The night before the trip I gave a farewellin party for my friends—a type of mountain celebratory event I learned about at Mount Everest. My trek party hosts at Everest feted their climbers with a get-together sendoff after our successful trip, just before we departed for home. I imported this excellent idea to Columbus, Indiana as an example of Hoosier hospitality. A crowd of family and friends showed up for pizza, beer, and story-telling. This turned out to the first of many farewellin send-offs for me—lucky climber that I am.

As Dom and I talked in the car on the way to Indianapolis International Airport the next morning, I knew the time for celebration had come to an end. Now, all the training I invested in would come to play. I thought, "Dear God, I remember the prayer in Genesis 24/12 made to you by Abraham's servant. Grant me success today, and for this entire expedition."

Parting is sweet sorrow.

Dom dropped me at the airport. When next I saw him and his lovely wife Kathryn, their lovely firstborn child, Siena, would have been baptized. I would still be in Africa for that event, and I hated the timing. Dom apologized, because I had delayed my departure to Kili to make sure I'd be home when Siena was born, having made my plane and trip reservations before learning Kathryn was pregnant. Then the impatient little girl decided to arrive early. Too funny. Yet I felt sad about missing the sacred occasion.

I checked in at Continental Airlines. The counter clerk, seeing my ticket's destination, told me he'd seen Kili from the Kenyan side of the mountain. He said, "Kilimanjaro has one 'foot' in Kenya and the other in Tanzania." Then the alert airline clerk noticed the poster on my backpack. With the help of administrative assistant Brittany Herche at St. Vincent Jennings, I had created a poster with a picture of Kilimanjaro. Words on the poster included basic info about where I was from, who I represented, and that I was raising money for youth obesity prevention and treatment.

I kept that poster on the pack for months, wore it each day while training, and found it drew constant attention. The airline clerk particularly noticed the last minute addendum sticky note I taped onto the bottom corner. I'd written "Psalm 46 /10" on the note.

He said, "What's that?"

I responded: "Oh, it's a favorite verse of mine from Psalms. It goes like this. 'Be still and know...' and then before I could say the rest, the clerk completed the verse saying: '...and know that I am God.'"

The Continental Airlines agent gave me a huge smile and waved me on, saying, "Have a great flight!" And we exchanged blessings. Did they even charge for my bags?

As a pastoral care hospital chaplain for St. Vincent with a post-graduate degree in theology who considers Psalms his favorite Biblical book, I found this was an especially beautiful way to begin the journey to my second of the Seven Summits. Psalm 46/10 is a verse I say every day. Even though I'm often in physical motion when I train, I may still quiet my mind and heart to "put God at the center," as my mentors Fr. Adrian VanKaam and Susan Muto taught me. I call this "meditation in motion" when simultaneously I trek and pray.

Coincidentally, I found that Psalm 46/10 is a woodcutting in relief outside the chapel at the St. Vincent Indianapolis Hospital. The woodcut is a production of Weberding Carving Shop. Bill

Weberding of the carving shop collaborated with me and with William Fenton, the St. Vincent Hospital Architect, on the Jennings chapel for which I was responsible. This gave the Psalms verse heightened meaning.

Before, during, and after the Indy airport, I used my St. Vincent Blackberry to send updates to Brittany at Jennings. Brittany helped me with Foundation activities and we collaborated on a blog sent to a growing list of people, including donors, prospective donors, and friends of our youth obesity program. This would allow them to "trek and climb along with Walter" in Africa. As I tried to get all this correspondence done, being inexperienced with a Blackberry and its tiny keys, I found my stubby little fingers often tangled with each other. Arrgh. Finally the blog update was complete, more or less.

From Indy I flew to Newark, New Jersey. This all went smoothly and my next stop would be Amsterdam. We left Newark at 6:30 p.m. for an 8 a.m. arrival in Holland.

Wednesday, 10 June, 2009

On the ground at Schiphol Airport in Amsterdam, I met Stan from North Carolina and his daughter Katie. They spotted my backpack poster and wanted to talk, as they were also en route to Kilimanjaro for a climbing adventure. Joining them would be Stan's other daughter Victoria, a Peace Corps volunteer. They believed they would be on my route, the Machame route. We talked about Kilimanjaro and home.

The poster attracted more Kili trekkers. Denise and Vic were from Cincinnati, only an hour from my hospital ministry in North Vernon. Their Ohio municipality and the teeny Hoosier town are connected by U.S. Highway 50. They too were Kilimanjaro bound. One of their sons was a music professor at IUPUI, Indiana

University-Purdue University at Indianapolis, 45 minutes from my home. This was almost like visiting with neighbors. To laughter, I told them all, "You have to go to Amsterdam to have a conversation about Kilimanjaro." We all spoke of what a small world this is. Other than my friend David in Columbus, who has the mission field in Ghana, I had found no one with whom to speak knowledgeably about Kili. But half a world away, people "got it," and were even "doing it."

I've found that my natural curiosity, along with my journalism training helps me socially when on my travels. I hear interesting answers to my questions that shape the world into a smaller place. When one knows a little geography, can remember information about people and places, and moreover knows how to conversationally connect the dots, the world is indeed a small place.

From Amsterdam, I traveled on to Kilimanjaro. Again we were blessed with an on-time and smooth flight. We landed about 8 p.m. Kilimanjaro time, having left Amsterdam about 10:30 that morning. Kilimanjaro International Airport, only three degrees south of the equator, felt steamy and hot, even at 8 p.m.

We needed to fill out and pay for Tanzanian visa paperwork. In the processing line I met another Cincy woman, this one a pediatrician from the University of Cincinnati Children's Hospital who was on a missionary trip with her mother in support of their Lutheran Church. She had climbed Kili maybe five years earlier. Again, the backpack poster did its thing to broadcast my mission and attract attention. The Cincy pediatrician said obesity was a "scourge" to young people and she appreciated what I was doing to help.

From the airport we had bumpy, hot, dusty ride in the dark to the village of Moshi where I would be staying at the Springlands Hotel. Did the ride take two hours or did it just seem that way? No stops, nor did I see any place to halt. Were lions or other predators lurking in the bush along the roadside I wondered? Good thing we didn't stop, I suppose.

The Springlands Hotel was an oasis emerging from the dark and dust and accumulated hours of travel. Check-in was smooth, and I reflected the whole trip has gone seamlessly. None of the airline, airport, or baggage glitches that tangled me up on the Everest expedition 24 months earlier. I thanked God for what some of my friends pray for, calling them "travel mercies."

Since the airport I'd been hearing the pleasant sound of African voices speaking English, and sometimes another language—Swahili, I believed. Perhaps they were also speaking other African languages. My new friend from North Carolina had his regional speech, as did my new friends from Cincy. Their accents I already knew—and liked. Ah, but the sounds of Tanzanians at Kili International and here at the Springlands were new, and so pleasant to the ear.

I felt tired, but not sleepy. After checking in and dropping my luggage in the room, I headed out to get a sandwich and a beer. The bar was empty and warm inside, so I strolled out to a cluster of tables and umbrellas set in a garden. I ordered a toasted cheese sandwich, which is about all that was available "this late," and a Kilimanjaro brand beer with a picture of the mountain on it.

Two women at a nearby table invited me to join them. They were from the Black Forest area of Germany, and we talked mountain talk. Their expedition would leave the next day and they would go on safari when they returned. "Sounds interesting," I said, but I said I'd declined the safari part. I would spend two weeks for the climb. I'd gotten homesick at Everest after being gone almost a month, so I figured I didn't need extra time on safari, although I hoped to see some of Africa's big animals. I said, "Still, I'm grateful the sightings didn't happen on the drive in from the airport."

They laughed and nodded in agreement.

The women excused themselves, turning in early for their big day. I headed to my room also, but ran across a group of guys at another table who invited me to sit with them. There were five young men, a trio from Norway, and two Brits—Martin and Josh. It turned out the three of us would be climbing together. They struck me as delightful young men and I hoped this would prove a blessing. My hopes would be realized.

Thursday, 11 June, 2009

My sleep wasn't refreshing that night, though usually I sleep like a little boy. Maybe this had something to do with the mosquito net surrounding the bed. New for me. Oh, well.

After breakfast, I had several objectives that included collecting my rental mountain gear. But the gear could wait. First, I needed and wanted to connect with some special people. That morning I had two important meetings. I would meet my mountain guide, Godlisten (yes, Godlisten was his given name), and I learned he'd be returning that day after leading a group up the mountain for the past two weeks. I talked to the Springslands staff after breakfast, learned of his return around lunchtime, and asked if I might meet him. They predicted that would be fine.

Before that, I would make the acquaintance of a special young man named David—an unexpected blessing that parachuted into my life as I prepared for Kilimanjaro. Kendall Wildey, one of the Jennings Hospital Foundation Board members, "introduced" me to David, at least to his name, at one of our meetings about the Kili fund raising initiative and program start-up.

Kendall said his church, the First Christian Church in North Vernon, sponsored a young man in Africa through its mission outreach program to help pay his way through school. Kendall knew David lived in Tanzania but didn't know exactly where. He asked me to contact his church youth ministry program for more information on the lad, whose name was David. I told Kendall I'd be happy to do so, but I believed Tanzania was three or more times the size of Indiana, (or was it Texas?), and not to get his hopes up.

"Just call Angee Leeds at First Christian and see what you can find out," were Kendall's parting words.

And so I called Angee and found out she was a delightful and high energy young woman. She didn't know where in Tanzania David lived, but said she'd find out. I repeated to her the remark about Indiana /Texas. Undaunted, she said she'd call me back after speaking with the intermediary stateside agency in Colorado that handled these relationships.

I'm sure I said a prayer about this possibility as I continued with my mountain preparations, not to mention doing my ministry at St. Vincent Jennings. As a part of the ministry, I needed to balance fundraising for the youth obesity program through the Foundation, seeing patients, and a gazillion other duties. Money had started to come in for youth obesity prevention and the treatment clinic already. Praise the Lord, and rock and roll.

When Angee called back after talking to Colorado, a God thing was about to unfold. First, imagine maps of Africa you have seen— the sheer size of the continent and its land mass. Imagine its many countries. There was Tanzania itself, definitely twice, or thrice, the size of Indiana (or Texas). Imagine the countless villages and towns in Indiana and multiply that by two or three. All the continental landmass of Africa and all its people, imagine! Imagine also that God had a plan for David and for me.

Angee said, "I hope this will help. David lives in the village of Moshi. That's where he goes to school."

"Moshi?" I stammered.

I was absolutely dumbfounded! David lived in the very village where I would be spending the two nights before our climb of Kilimanjaro! Unbelievable. Well, not really.

"Angee, I don't know if you're ready for this, so buckle up. David lives in precisely the town I will be staying in before we go to the mountain!" I said excitedly.

"God thing," she simply said.

So Angee and the First Christian Church and their intermediary in Denver arranged for me to meet David. We were about to spend 90 minutes together in the hotel's garden commons gathering area, where I met Martin and Josh the night before.

The hotel staff alerted me my guests had arrived and I would need to meet them at the gate. For security reasons, a locked gate surrounded our hotel. This wasn't how I wished to meet a special guest, but security was security. I verified my guests to the attendant.

David was escorted in by his school's headmaster, who spoke English. David's grandmother accompanied him, as did a school social worker. A second social worker would join us later.

David was about half my height, a lithe lad of three feet tall who may have weighed 50 pounds. He was ten years old, having celebrated his birthday a few days earlier. He wore a pressed yellow dress shirt with cuff links. I expected he dressed up for the occasion. He wore long pants. His ebony skin and dark, shining eyes contrasted with his shirt. He made eye contact with me, but was quiet and seemed shy. I am Italian and hug naturally, but wisdom prompted me to be reserved. I didn't know the customs. To bring us eye to eye, I knelt down and shook David's hand lightly. I shook hands with his grandmother, who had a beautiful face. Taller than me, she wore a turban made from the same material as her stunning full length dress. She stood straight and tall. Neither David nor his grandmother spoke English. The headmaster, whose name also was David, spoke English fluently, as did the social workers.

Surprisingly, each adult gave me a hug.

We sat in the garden area under a roofed structure and began our visit. I explained how both the mountain and youth obesity brought me to Africa. Kilimanjaro they knew, of course. The puzzlement in their faces about youth obesity was my first brush with a misunderstanding that would occur every time I told native Tanzanians about my cause. It took me awhile to realize the cause: Africa has a chronic food shortage. Most of the native citizens walk everywhere because they have little access to, nor ownership, of motorized transportation. The natives have zero problems with youth obesity. They have little to eat, and they exercise. Those are fundamental parts of their lives—like breathing.

I wanted to know about my new young friend and asked if I might ask him some questions. Shy at first, and a little in awe of my attention toward him, David began to warm up, his bright eyes shining. He made good grades in school, I learned. I asked of his future aspirations after school, if he had any. This was translated to him by the headmaster as were all my questions, and then his answers translated to me.

"Yes, he does," the headmaster said. "When he grows up he would like to be a soldier." Then the headmaster paused. "Wait. That is wrong. I misunderstood." He and David conversed some more in Swahili. Correcting himself, the headmaster said, "Not a soldier. What David wants to be is a journalist. You know—write for newspapers or magazines."

My mouth dropped open and I said, "Yes, I know journalism. That is how I trained and what I did after college."

We all remarked at the coincidence, including a smile from David when his headmaster relayed this information.

I changed the subject, directing everyone's attention, especially David's, to parcels concealed under the table. I had come bearing gifts and wished to present them to David.

A packet of many letters individually addressed to David came from the First Christian Church youth ministry kids. Angee had each child at the church write David a personal letter, and I served as the postman. The church also sent another gift: A bright red shirt which in big white lettering said: First Christian Church, North Vernon, Indiana, USA.

I motioned David to put this on over his dress shirt and helped him do so. I knew the church would want a photo of this! Good choice Angee Leeds, to choose a T-shirt and have it made in red. David looked so cool in the shirt. Home run! David, his grandmother, and the school officials all beamed at this gift.

I had asked my hospital's Mission Team to contribute one of the backpacks of school supplies we give kids in need at the beginning of each school year. This project was begun by Cindy Corya and Terry Everage of the hospital staff as their Mission and Mentoring project. It grew from ten backpacks given out the first year, to almost 500 a year. The hospital distributes these gifts to children whose families can't afford backpacks or the school supplies to put in them. As the project grew, merchants and other groups joined the hospital in this effort. Starting with Jennings county impoverished kids, we grew to international distribution.

David looked at the packet of letters, all addressed to him and I think the look he gave me was disbelief and sheer gratitude. And then he looked inside the backpack and stared at me as though I'd given him gold coins. To this young man an abundance of everyday school supplies was treasure. The things we Westerners take for granted, thought I. He found another T-shirt, one from the United Way of Jennings County.

The items inside the back pack included a notepad of paper in the shape of the St. Vincent Doves logo. He and his support crew delighted in the story of the St. Vincent Doves logo. I explained about the body-mind-spirit connection and the doves flying in integrated formation, symbolic of the balance we should feel among each of these realms within our life. We were late on the calendar for his birthday as it turned out, but David had received a load of useful loot and personal communication from North Vernon, Indiana, USA, all the way to Moshi, Tanzania, Africa. What an auspicious beginning to my time in Africa.

Then my new-found friends turned the tables on me.

"And we wish to gift you with something," the headmaster said. "But first, we will honor the Tanzanian tradition of singing a song about gift giving and gift opening."

And they sang for me—loudly. This drew the attention of everyone who was out and about at the hotel. I didn't know the words, but their song had a lively melody and they all sang happily. I was now beaming, though a little embarrassed by the attention. The hotel staff all seemed to understand the words of the song and they were beaming too.

My beaming magnified in a moment, turning into gratitude, pride, and humility, as I opened a newspaper-wrapped gift. Their gift was a beautiful, homemade large Tanzanian shirt. Young David looked at me and gestured as if to say, "Put it on, just like I did my T-shirt." So I did—and the shirt was a perfect fit.

Now it was time for a photo shoot, but my new friends beat me to it by pulling out their camera first. Through the interpreter, I asked David if he'd want to sit by me for a picture. My desire not to break cultural barriers was still on my mind. He jumped right onto my lap and threw his arm affectionately around me. So much for cultural barriers. And we did a photo shoot all around.

Headmaster David then offered a prayer of thanksgiving for our time together, for my trek and safety, and for my fundraising initiative.

I bought bottled water for them, but, as coached, I didn't offer to pay their expenses to the hotel, whatever that might have been. Angee instructed me to this attention to detail through the Denver intermediary. Should I ask them to stay for lunch and treat them? But what about meeting my guide Godlisten? Conflict of times the clock told me, but I held my tongue. Headmaster David gave me the polite out, saying he knew I had much to attend to.

What began with a handshake ended with hugs to all, including young David. *Thank you God for this time together.* I walked David and his grandmother and the entourage to the gate to bid them farewell. We all smiled at each other and waved.

When I returned to the commons garden area to pick up after us, I saw Linda, a supervisor I met earlier in the morning. She smiled and asked, "Would you like to meet Godlisten? He's back from the mountain."

Oh, my—perfect timing.

Godlisten shook my hand and gave me a hug that he initiated, like David and crew. He had just now returned from summiting a group atop Uhuru Peak at 19,340 feet the morning before. His group strolled into the common garden area with him, but just for now, he invited me to sit down so we might visit. We sat down together and immediately I felt caught up by his eye contact, his warm engaging manner, his ability to listen and not interrupt, his accent and beautiful manner of speaking English. He let me buy him a beverage and chose a Nehi Orange Crush, a soda from my kidhood days.

We sat close, closer than might be comfortable back home; although I wasn't in the least uncomfortable with our proximity. I was struck by how he listened, and listened, and listened more. He was so very cordial to me, while also being courteous to his climbing group. During our time together, perhaps every ten minutes, he excused himself to see to his group. The cordial and easy way he did this I found respectful, and not at all disconcerting. We visited for about 20 minutes.

I had chosen Godlisten to be my guide and requested him from his Zara organization on the basis of his name. I reference checked him with previous clients, each of whom gave highest marks. No disrespect to "Photo Joe" or other Zara guides whom I'm sure do competent jobs, but my thinking was: "Walter, you're a pastoral care hospital chaplain bringing God to people. Look at that name. It says: Godlisten."

When I saw this name I wondered, "What were his parents thinking? His name surely is indicative of who and what he represents. Godlisten will make a great expedition greater." I shared this with friends at home, and everyone was intrigued by the name. Some friendly doubters teased me, suggesting I made up his name.

"Who has a name like that?"

My response to them was simple. I said, "That will be my first question to Godlisten on meeting him. I will ask: 'What were your parents thinking when they named you?'"

And when Godlisten rejoined me at our table after checking on his crew, I asked that question. He smiled, then grew more serious, and said: "My parents wanted me to have a relationship with the Divine. So they gave me this name. When I write my name, when I read my name, when I say my name, when others say my name, I am reminded of my relationship with the Almighty. My family wanted me to remember this always—my relationship. With God. And so they gave me this name. And so I am reminded and I remember."

I found his answer simple and eloquent. His mountaineering and guiding skills were extraordinary. Godlisten had climbed Kilimanjaro 150 plus times, he said. He was well known and respected on the mountain. This would become evident to me, as it seemed all the Tanzanians knew him. By his name. And most of the locals abbreviated it to "God-y."

I found the story of his name so compelling. Beyond his explanation, I remain touched by what it combined: God's name ... connected to the attribute of listening. His parents didn't name their son "Godtalker." They accented listening. Many people I know actively "talk to" or "talk at" God. How few of them, including me oftentimes, take time to listen to God? Gody's compound blending of the name and attribute was a wonderful theological teaching.

Before Gody excused himself he taught me a few Swahili phrases—encouraging words and phrases of greeting.

From the time I met David and his crew and talked to Gody, perhaps two hours had passed. I was absolutely riveted by my new friends from Africa. This was a holy time, and the ground we were on felt sacred. Perhaps even the chairs where I parked my butt were holy too. Well, Gody's chair for sure.

Tomorrow was our departure day for Kilimanjaro and I still needed climbing gear, so I reported to the gear shop at the other end of the grounds and greeted the supervisor Linda, who introduced me to Mary, who helped me collect what I needed: a down sleeping bag, puffy below-zero parka jacket, expedition bag, trek poles, and so on. While there, I talked with the 25-year-old Brits, Martin and Josh, whom I met the previous night. They were also collecting their "kits" as they called the pack and contents. Very pleasant "chaps," again using their vernacular.

Friday, 12 June, 2009

I enjoyed a wonderful sleep, thanks God. Rolling out of the sack, I read Bible verses from the mini-Bible I carried in my backpack, read my friend Rabbi Arnold's Jewish Travel Prayer for Safety, shaved, did some journaling, conducted a final check of my pack, reviewed my expedition bag contents, and headed to breakfast.

At the forefront of my mind was this: I had trained for this day non-stop since the beginning of October—eight months earlier. I considered myself as fit as I'd ever been in my life, because I trained virtually every day for 240 days. Columbus' Mill Race Park and its 100-foot high observation tower became the centerpiece of my training efforts. My thanks to the Force family and the Schumaker family, both of Columbus, who sponsored the tower, and to the City of Columbus Parks and Recreation Department which maintains it. Along with Mill Race's Ampitheater Earthen Mound and the Parks' fine system of People Trails, I had good facilities near my home for training. And the hills of Brown County at the state park and my son Andy's hilly property were only 15 miles farther west.

I reflected on highlights from tower training before Martin and Josh joined me for breakfast. First, I was vigilant about visiting the tower almost every day to get a vertical mile going up and down. My friends' math and engineering might have been a little imprecise, but Greg Scherschel and Dana North calculated that five trips up and down equaled one linear mile. I wore my trek boots and carried a pack that weighed 25 to 30 pounds for the five circuits, nearly seven days a week. The mile took 20 minutes. My linear or level ground miles took 20 minutes. This gave me confidence in my ability to go up and down at a reasonable pace.

Second, on one weekend I did 15 trips in one go on the tower, which further boosted my confidence. The third tower highlight was the WISH Indianapolis Channel Eight clip of my training on the tower.

The station was generous in reporting the story of my fundraising efforts for youth obesity at St. Vincent Jennings. They aired the clip in conjunction with my participation in the Indianapolis Mini Marathon. I was training for my 50th mini, this one completed while walking in trek boots and carrying my backpack, on Saturday after they aired the feature news clip about me.

WISH's news coverage provided some balm to the hurt I felt after corporate public relations at St. Vincent Indianapolis ignored my request for news media support of the fundraiser.

As I told Joe Roche, my Jennings CEO: "If I were an Indianapolis physician or associate or volunteer paying his or her own way to Africa to climb Kilimanjaro and raise money for a St. Vincent Indianapolis program—can you imagine the news media support I would have received, and the financial gifts?" That was the first of several rebuff or dismissive feelings I received as corporate PR looked the other way to support other causes closer to Indianapolis.

This became a lesson in controlling things I could control, like my training, and letting go of what I couldn't control.

The Mill Race and Brown county training venues had me as physically prepared as a flatlander Hoosier headed to Kili could be. By contrast, I was 61 years old and my new friends from England, Martin and Josh, age 25, were both younger than my sons.

My training consisted of an early morning trek of two to three miles. A "trek," by my definition, meant I wore the Scarpa brand trek boots I'd worn to Everest and would wear also for Kilimanjaro. It also meant I wore my backpack with at least 25 pounds of weight, clean kitty litter. Why kitty litter? Because it's well packaged and easier to handle than dumb bell weights or books. Sometimes I added rocks or cans of soda to incrementally increase the weight. Each day I included 20 or more minutes, going up or down stairs or hills, in my boots, carrying the loaded pack. At least a vertical mile each day was the minimum I'd need for the African mountain. At lunch time I often used the stairwell steps at St. Vincent Jennings next door to the chapel. I climbed these steps from the ground level four floors up, and back down. Muscatatuck Park in North Vernon with its hills was another lunchtime favorite.

When I left for Kilimanjaro I believed I was stronger than when I left for Everest. Training also meant paying careful attention to hydration, especially on long weekend treks to the hills of Brown County State Park, or at son Andy and his wife Jill's home and property in the upland area of Brown County. To avoid the medical issues that beset me at Everest, I promised myself every day I would drink three liters of water, mixed with Gatorade. Often in my training treks I used trek poles, as I would be using these on the mountain.

Training became more challenging and tough as I increased my distance and pack weight. Apart from training, funds weren't being raised for the youth obesity program as rapidly as I'd hoped. This latter development was complicated by what I regarded as the inadequate public relations support from St. Vincent Indianapolis, for whatever reason. No one else in Indiana was climbing mountains to raise money for youth obesity, or any other purpose. It wasn't in our Hoosier psyche. Yet, people all said my idea was innovative and unique. Naively, I suppose I thought because we had something unique and creative, the support would be forthcoming. With the push in training levels, tepid fundraising, and hospital politics, my spirits sank.

Amid that backdrop, when my spirits were flagging, I got a call to drop by Human Resources at Jennings.

My friend Kathryn Johnson was waiting for me. I must have been wearing my feelings on my sleeve, as apparently I looked a little wane and Kathryn commented on it. I lamented my training tiredness and frustration with St. Vincent Indianapolis. Kathryn commiserated. Then, she shifted gears. Kathryn was the head of HR as well as PR for St. Vincent Jennings.

She beamed: "Well, I have a surprise I think you'll like. I have some information from Virgin Health Miles that concerns you. And I believe you'll feel better after you hear it."

Virgin Health Miles (VHM), part of the Virgin group of companies owned by explorer and entrepreneur Richard Branson was the corporate wellness program with which St. Vincent contracted. Richard Branson was Sir Richard, in fact, as the British royals had knighted him. St. Vincent used VHM to encourage associates to exercise to get in shape, stay fit, and be well. Associates received "awards" of merchandise options or cash for the exercise they did. VHM gave each of us a clip-on pedometer called a Go Zone to track steps and miles, time invested in exercise, and calories burned. This information could be downloaded from the pedometer into a computer program for tracking purposes.

Earlier, I had sought VHM as a corporate sponsor of my climb and asked them for a healthy donation to help us fund the youth obesity clinic at St. Vincent Jennings. They said they'd consider it and get back to me. After several weeks I received an update call telling me to be patient, as they were still considering my request. Several more weeks passed and I wondered if they'd forgotten me—or rejected me without the courtesy of a notification.

Kathryn in HR knew more than I did. "You know how you asked Virgin Health Miles to sponsor you for your Trek for Kids for youth obesity to Mount Kilimanjaro? Well they've done more than just sponsor you."

"What do you mean?" I asked, not understanding.

"Well, they're going to do a number of things for you. First, they've created a new national award to recognize someone who models and promotes wellness. And they thought, considering what you're doing with Mount Kilimanjaro and youth obesity here at the hospital, that you should be the inaugural recipient."

I looked at Kathryn blankly, silent and dumbfounded.

Scarcely pausing for a breath, she continued, "Step two, they also created a competition between our associates to occur while you're on the mountain. They will match, up to a $1,000, the step output of our associates.

"And, third, they want us, here at Jennings, as well as at St. Vincent 86th Street at Indy," Kathryn looked at me knowingly and for emphasis repeated, "and at St. Vincent 86th Street, to publicize what they're doing in connection with you. How about that? How do you feel now?" Kathryn joyfully asked.

I was beyond shocked. I felt humbled. I felt grateful. And, I was tearful. You could have pushed me over with a feather.

Kathryn informed me the national award, titled Eye on Wellness, would be given annually to an individual recipient and to a corporate recipient. The awards would be announced in the spring during National Employee Wellness Month. "These awards will commend an individual and a corporation shown to be outstanding wellness advocates and role models for others," Virgin Health Miles said in its notification to Kathryn.

To say I gave my Kathryn a giant hug would be an understatement.

Virgin Health Miles put a big PR splash on its web site about the award and carried a write up and pics about 2Trek4Kids, and about my climb up Kilimanjaro.

In their documents, which needed to be signed by representatives of St. Vincent, as well as myself, they directed St. Vincent to publicize my initiative and, of course, mention Virgin Health Miles. For my part, I agreed to donate a year's worth of my cash awards to the youth obesity prevention and treatment clinic getting started at Jennings. As I had already committed to doing this, I smiled at their request. In fact, all the cash awards I earned through Virgin Health Miles over the years were divided between and among what would become three youth obesity prevention and treatment programs at St. Vincent Jennings, Salem, Indiana, and Dunn Hospital in Bedford, Indiana.

For this first fundraiser, Virgin Health Miles created the Walter Verses the World Step Competition, involving our Jennings associates competing against each other. This fun competition ended with Virgin Health Miles donating $1,000 to the St. Vincent Jennings youth obesity program.

As a salve to my angst, St. Vincent Indianapolis paid attention and devoted recognition to what was happening at Jennings around youth obesity, thanks to contributions from Kathryn, and thanks to Jon White at St. Vincent 86th Street Corporate PR.

Those 20 minutes with Kathryn Johnson that afternoon, when training had stiffened and people who mattered were insensitive, transformed everything to good in a moment of grace.

Virgin Health Miles, Sir Richard Branson's company, and him an explorer I admired, had remembered me. Instead of my hopes for youth obesity prevention and treatment being consigned to the rejection heap, the initiative was honored in a greater way than I imagined. This provided impetus and propulsion to help me reach a higher level for training, and for creating awareness about youth obesity.

With my own background in hospital public relations, I began finding opportunities to contact news media on my own about the upcoming trek. Bryce Mayer at *The Plain Dealer* in North Vernon was generous with news coverage. Reporters for *The Columbus Republic* newspaper Sunday edition for Jennings County got interested, as did Mary Ann Wyand at *The Criterion* Catholic

Archdiocesan newspaper for central and southern Indiana. A news and camera crew for WISH TV in Indianapolis did a lengthy segment set in Mill Race Park on prime time news. Barb Berggoetz at *The Indianapolis Star* did a nice profile.

And somehow I found new physical strength that resulted in a PR (personal record) mark on the Mill Race Tower.

Oh, yes, where would the fund-raising initiative be without our donors, including Virgin Health Miles. Thus I remembered all these generous and wonderful people, too—God bless them please.

These were some of the things on my mind as Martin and Josh sat down with me at "breaky," as they called breakfast. A little later we sat down together again, after boarding a small bus bound for the Machame Gate Entrance to Mount Kilimanjaro.

Now I would view the village of Moshi for the first time, since we had arrived in the dark. Daylight revealed what we would label poverty back home, but was it so here? I carried a Western perspective and baggage of expectation. I reminded myself, perhaps the standard of living was simply lower and the citizens didn't consider themselves poor. Housing appeared substandard compared to back home, for sure. Markets, businesses, and petrol stations showed up in a scattered way. Buildings for business, government, and churches were clustered in the vicinity of a roundabout, with more people and vehicular traffic coming and going. As we neared the outskirts of town, Gody had the driver stop so the expedition stores could be fortified with fresh fruit. He suggested the climbers buy several chocolate bars, saying they'd be good for quick energy, most especially on the summit day.

When we drove out of town, the semi-paved roads went from pavement to a mix of road surfaces that always shared one thing in common: holes—many of them deep and wide enough to rattle our bones. Tall stands of corn began appearing on the hillsides.

Clouds hid the sky and the mountain from view as we approached. Funny thing—as we moved closer, the bus started going downhill. I learned later the weight of the gigantic land mass of Kilimanjaro, according to geologists and geophysicists, was so heavy it created a great depression in the earth.

We travelled perhaps an hour from the hotel to the entrance of the national park gate where our trek and climb would begin.

As the bus slowed to a stop, butterflies fluttered through my inner calm. I smiled and remembered Columbus politico Robert Garton's words: "Butterflies are okay. Just teach 'em to fly in formation." I gently re-centered myself with focus.

Foremost in my mind were the kids who would benefit from the program, their families, and the compassionate and competent clinicians who would support them. Also atop my mind was my safety, my hopes to summit, the spiritual dimension of the climb, and the hope of making new friends. Great blessings awaited me— but let me not get ahead of myself.

We left the bus to join Gody and his crew, who awaited us at the foot of the rain forest at the Machame Gate. As if on cue, rain began to fall. Ahead of us were muddy slick spots and wet everything from the rain, heat, and humidity. The foliage and plants I saw as we unloaded the gear had a lush, damp, tropical beauty. As we ascended, this show of nature would only improve.

Our crew of porters had organized our personal gear and "community gear" from the bus and parceled it into manageable loads. The community gear contained items that would serve us on the climb, including lodging tents, toilet tents, dining tents, food, our expedition bags, mountain gear, and personal items. Unbelievably, our porters planted the loads on their heads and started up the trail ahead of us. Their strength and balance was awesome. We carried our own backpacks containing what we expected to need for a day's trek, including food and water. Water for me meant the three liters I fully intended to consume each day. The water added weight, so when all was said and done, I was at my 25 pound pack training weight. Each of us also packed an expedition bag full of other personal items carried by crew members.

While we waited, I chatted with my new friends Martin and Josh. I'd just met our other trekker couple—Chris and Yosra, newlyweds on their honeymoon to summit Kilimanjaro. Godlisten greeted me warmly; he would be guiding me, and each of the pairs had their own guide.

The trail through the rain forest was well established and easy to follow, snaking up and up the mountain. The narrow, dark brown, wet and muddy trail passed through a dense forest full of green vegetation with trees everywhere, many wearing grayish moss coats and accented in heather.

We were on the Machame route, nicknamed the Whiskey Route, and described in the literature as the most arduous and beautiful trail on the mountain. The trail followed a kind of zig-zag pattern up the mountain, switch-backing here and there. We didn't simply go straight up as on The Incline near Manitou Springs, Colorado. The switchbacks were a good thing, allowing us to conserve energy while not going too high too quickly, which would produce elevation sickness.

The rain forest was steamy, hot, and humid. As soon as the rain stopped I quickly slipped out of my poncho. I wore shorts, a Virgin Health Miles T-shirt, and an Indianapolis Mini Marathon baseball cap to which I pinned a kerchief to keep the sun off my neck. I didn't need the kerchief so much now, because the rain forest, so named for the abundance of rainfall at this level, was a dark forest, enchanting to walk through. The sun couldn't pierce the natural canopy of vegetation overhead. Our climb started on a four wheel drive track that soon slimmed to a narrow single person trail. From that point it was only for people going one way—up. No descents from here on. The higher up we went, the more interesting became the botanic spectacle, especially the red and yellow Impatiens Kilimanjaro, which has more than 1,000 species. Thousands of plant varieties live on Kilimanjaro and nowhere else, thanks to the mountain's rich volcanic soil, abundant rainfall, frost, and heat from the equator. Monkeys scampered overhead in the trees, but I heard them more than saw them.

When we stopped for a lunch, Godlisten warned me to keep food close and wrapped up because sneaky varmit rodents might try to liberate it from me. Again, I visited with Martin and Josh. These pleasant young men came from the London area and we shared an interest in tennis. Martin was a follower of the Wimbeldon Grand Slam event that would be played in a few weeks. He was a military air traffic controller. As I remember, Josh worked for his church. Chris and Yosra were pleasant. He was an international citizen having lived many places, and she was Egyptian. I asked about her name and I believe I understood her to say—"Gift from God from suffering." I expected there was a story behind her name and made a mental note to ask her sometime.

I kept drinking and drinking and drinking, determined to consume three liters of water a day. I also reminded myself about "Poley, poley," which, translated from Swahili to English, means "Slowly, slowly." The idea is to ascend at a measured pace to avoid altitude sickness. My intentions around hydration and pace would help avoid the illness I experienced at Everest. Saying, and hearing others say, "Poley poley" was an excellent verbal cue.

I took a prescription drug, Diamox, as I did at Everest to help with breathing the thin air up high. I also carried the rescue steroid, Dexamethasone, to use if I got into serious trouble. Needing the Dex would be a signal to end my climb and head down. The prescription meds were a blessing from Dr. Jones, an Indianapolis physician I met while getting ready for Everest—an elevation and mountain physician. He was knowledgeable, friendly, accessible, and had a keen sense of humor,

The rain forest is also called the Cloud Forest, as of course rain and clouds go hand in hand. Today's showers stopped shortly after we began our trek upward. It wasn't as though we were ascending through cloud layers, but I would come to better understand this name as we climbed higher on the mountain and saw a cloud deck beneath us.

During our first day we went uphill for five hours, which amounted to seven miles. I hydrated as planned and walked slowly, keeping an even, moderate pace. When we were finished I was pleasantly tired, but not overwhelmingly fatigued.

A surprise developed on the mountain. Godlisten and I walked together a fair bit, but he also spent time walking with the entire crew of guides and porters whom he oversaw. At one point when we walking together, he surprised me by calling me "Papa Walter." Noticing this, two other guides who were nearby also started calling me "Papa Walter." I wasn't sure how to feel. I didn't say anything, but I sure did notice. "Papa Walter" ...Hmm! What to make of that, I wondered?

Another surprise awaited me in our camp. Each of our three little climber groups, with me being solo, had our own small dining tent with a table and chairs. And each of our groups, plus me, had our own little toilet tent complete with a small chemical toilet. Oh, my goodness. I hadn't expected such luxuries.

Josh and Martin, being from London, christened their dining tent with the name of the famous luxury hotel The Ritz at Picadilly, and even put a sign on the front flap declaring it such. They kindly invited me over to have dinner with them, seeing as I was alone. They proved to be individually and collectively funny, sarcastic, engaging, good story tellers, and fine listeners. We had a delightful meal and evening together. And another surprise unfolded at dinner when the trekking crew acted as waiters and brought our food to us. "Maybe this is the Ritz!" I exclaimed.

The crew members were so kind—aiming to please. They brought us courses, tea first or something else to drink if we wished; fresh fruit next, which always seemed to include tiny African bananas along with other local fare; then a big plate or bowl of whatever was being served, a kind of stew that first night with fresh vegetables. I wasn't sure what the meat was. I had eaten gazelle at the hotel restaurant and found it absolutely delicious. Helpings were plentiful and seconds followed if we wished. Then something sweet arrived for dessert. More tea was served all along the way and to finish with, of course. It seemed the crew scurried to and fro like we were in the finest of restaurants. Rain began falling sometime during dinner.

As I went to bed, I reflected that today had special meaning on the calendar for me—my mom's birthday. It was also the day in 1957 that my dad died. Yes, he died on my mom's birthday at age 57, at home in bed. I was age nine when this happened. Mom lived into the 1990s. I doubt if I ever sensitively explored what it was like for Mom having her husband die on her birthday. One of our family rules seemed to be not talking much about those who died.

People dying and death, especially the death of children who predeceased their parents, became a focal point of my pastoral care ministry. I companioned people who were dying and their families. I have been a part of four groups for moms and dads and families of children who died before their parents. Sadly, what I learned to do for others, I didn't know how to do for my mom.

Dad's death from a heart attack came 40 years before my mom died. Thus, she was a widow a long time. She was just entering middle age when dad died, and I was still a boy, so I hardly got to know him. His name was John Thomas Glover. There was a book about a president entitled, "Johnny, We Hardly Knew Ye." The book title summed up a lot about my relationship with my father.

In my bedroll in the tent that night, listening to the rain outside, I remembered something the only living relative on dad's side had told me. As he had actually known my dad, I gave it great credence. While I prepared for Everest, my cousin Karl e-mailed me that my dad was "Adventuresome ... widely-traveled and world-curious." Karl said he "had no doubt that this was firmly imprinted" in me.

That made me smile. "Thank you, Mom, and thank you Dad, for my life and for my names. And I closed my eyes for sleep. "P.S.— happy birthday, Mom!" Today, after all, was her day, and it was Dad's day too. Some faith traditions say your death date, when you meet your Maker at the Pearly Gates, hopefully is when you become a saint stepping into God's presence in Heaven.

The rain was brisk and I decided to sleep in my clothes outside the bedroll, as that felt comfortable. But when Mother Nature woke me to take a leak, I felt cold. When I went outside to relieve myself after the rain stopped, another surprise awaited: A clear, bejeweled night sky, vibrant with stars and the light of the near full moon ... and there way up in the distance was "the shining mountain," as the name Kilimanjaro is translated. I clearly saw its outlines and the glaciers capping it. *Oh my, Creator God Elohim. What a majestic sight.*

Saturday, 13 June, 2009

I had an excellent sleep, like a little boy. After my nocturnal introduction to The Shining Mountain, Kilimanjaro, "Kili" for short, and I had another face-to-face. I emerged from my cocoon of sleeping bag and tent into a sunny dawn. There the mountain stood in full daylight, unencumbered by clouds.

"Good morning, Kili! I see you in the distance. Soon I will see you up close and personal," I said. I was able to make out some of the mountain's features. "Isn't that the Western Breach?" I asked myself. Gody later confirmed it. The rubble of that vertical wall was created when the mountain collapsed on itself under the weight of lava flowing from the tremendous volcanic activity.

"Jambo, Jambo," Gody enthusiastically called, seeing me outside my tent. This was a greeting I came to love, because I'm all about being a morning person and love to greet and be greeted by "Good Morning!" Which is what "jambo" means in Swahili.

And Gody's voice wonderfully accented the Swahili, "Jambo, Papa Walter." Hmm, there was that name again.

Our trek soon got underway and we moved out of the rain forest, which formed a kind of belt surrounding the entire mountain and keeping it moist. The forest wrapped the mountain until we reached the heather and the grassy moorland zone. The going became steep for three hours, and stayed that way much of the day. I saw beautiful flowers, including the aptly called red hot poker, more Impatiens Kilimanjaro, lobelia, and senecio.

Uh oh, I also felt an onset of the "niggles" as the Brits and the locals hereabouts called the feeling related to diarrhea. This wasn't the full blown kind, thankfully. But it soon became annoying and necessitated a few stops along the trail. Thankfully the trail leveled out and I found plenty of huge boulders to lean against.

In level areas the trail widened, so Gody and I walked alongside one another and we talked. I found him to be a gentle, patient man. This belied his immense physical strength. I found his strength went beyond physical and was also emotional, mental, and spiritual.

Gody told me he was one of 11 children, three of whom were deceased. His parents were still living, his mom frail due to what sounded like arthritic and debilitating knees. Knee surgery would cost a fortune in schillings—completely out of the question. Gody's dad was unable to care for his wife due to his age, so she alternated between the adult children. Gody's siblings viewed him as the family leader, which created its own set of challenges. His (then) eight year old "beloved daughter" was in private school; her younger brother was in government school because Gody couldn't afford to send them both to private schools, which he said "are very expensive." Enamored by the quality of private school education, he scoffed at the public schools saying "Teachers are there just for the salary."

We reached Shira Camp at 12,621 feet. Machame Gate, where we began was 5,997 feet. Machame Huts, our first overnight camp where I first saw Kili's summit was 9,948 feet of elevation. We were moving up. We'd go further, God willing, to 19,340 feet and Uhuru Peak. Translated to English from Swahili, it means Independence Peak. This name was given the Roof of Africa after Tanzania claimed independence as a nation. So far, we'd progressed upward to double the elevation from where we began. We had entered and exited the wet, enchanted forest.

On this day we climbed steadily upward to come out on the plateau of the Shira Camp where we'd stay overnight. This day's trek was as dusty as yesterday was muddy and then green. Yet we saw wonderful botany, including giant groundsels called senecio Kilimanjaro and lobelias dotting our landscape. The day's heat made the climbing more challenging.

I began to see distinguishing rocks colored black, kind of like they were partially polished. They were called obsidian.

I collected small obsidian rocks, left over from the volcanic days of old. Kilimanjaro is made up of three volcanoes. Shira, where we were, was the rim of the oldest of Kili's three volcanoes. It is a collapsed ruin now, flattened, having fallen in on itself. Mount Meru was the second volcano to erupt. Kibo was the last to explode, rising on the shoulders of its siblings, higher than either of them. All this happened hundreds of thousands of years ago, the geophysicists say. The Rift Valley occupies this part of East Africa, which is home to countless "deceased" or inactive volcanoes that occurred with the separation of tectonic plates hundreds of miles beneath the surface of the earth. One day, geologists predict, East Africa may separate from its host continent as these volcanoes cause a separation, like a gulf, within the land mass.

Meantime, in the today of Creation, I collected yesterday's obsidian stones to carry home as souvenirs. If a black vehicle were waxed with a smudged or dirty cloth, it might give off the kind of dross shine Obsidian has.

Later, after arriving home, I passed out one my souvenir obsidian stones from hundreds of thousands of years ago at talks I gave to school and community groups. I asked them to "feel" Kilimanjaro as they passed the rock round a room, touching it. My purpose was to give them the tactile experience of actually touching history from the ancient continent of Africa.

My favorite story about obsidian concerns the only two people I met who recognized the stone. Remarkably, the first was a third grader in Janis Boyd's class at Scipio Grade School in Jennings County where I gave a presentation. The other was a PhD geologist named Michael Lewan in Denver, Colo., who is married to my dear lifetime friend Jeannie Becherer Lewan from Bedford, Indiana days in kindergarten, grade school and high school.

The stone made its rounds in Janis' class as I gave my talk on Kilimanjaro. When it reached one little girl, she thrust her hand high in the air to get my attention. When I called on her, she nearly jumped out of her chair to exclaim, I know what kind of stone this is!"

I hadn't given them the rock's geologic name, so I said, "Really. What?"

"Obsidian," she answered.

"You are so right!" I was so thrilled, I forgot to ask how she knew.

Later I visited Jeannie and Mike at their Colorado home, told this story, and held out the rock. Before I got to the naming part, Mike with his postgraduate degree and knowledge identified it correctly, of course, as obsidian. I told him the story about the pupil and asked, "How do you think she knew?"

Mike guessed, "I bet she and her family traveled to Hawaii and saw Hawaii's volcano and the same kind of obsidian stones, which are volcanic based rock. She learned it there I expect." Mystery solved.

On the third day's climb, Gody and I brought up the rear of our three groups as we neared the Shira Plateau and the spot where we'd camp overnight. Martin and Josh and their guide, and Chris and Yosra and their guide, were ahead of us, and had already arrived and dropped their packs—as I would soon learn. All of a sudden Martin showed up, having retreated about a quarter mile back to where Gody and I were still on the trail. Martin happily grabbed my back pack, saying jovially, "I thought maybe you could use a hand, Walter." I accepted his kindness receiving it as happily as he gave it. I didn't feel drained, but what a kind gesture by a kindly man.

As our three groups squared away in camp by mid-afternoon, my expedition partners and their guides were putting together a short trek about a half-hour away to the Shira caves; geologic depressions where Kili climbers once stayed overnight. It was said that some of Africa's big beasts, lions, also sought shelter there. I didn't know this at the time. My friends asked me to join them on their trek, and I did.

So I walked with four others and their guides away from our camp toward the Shira Caves about a mile away. On nearing the cave site, the niggles returned. Cramps were getting the better of me, so I had to seek relief. I told the group to go on and I would catch up with them. However, my relief stop took longer than expected and the group did as I said—they were out of sight. Darn. I didn't realize the mistake I had made, or its gravity.

I pretty much remembered the way we came and wasn't alarmed. In fact, I even did a little side trail exploring on the way back. The four others were already in camp when I returned. And Godlisten was waiting like an upset parent on the doorstep whose child has been where he shouldn't—and worse, was absent way too long.

Godlisten's voice changed. Stern and convicting like a judge, his message was firm and succinct: "You want to go somewhere, you find me and we will go there if it is safe. You don't leave and go off with others. You stay with me. You had no business there without me. Never be alone. There are lions about on this mountain. Do you agree with what I tell you?"

This was all about safety. Time and again Godlisten proved himself vigilant for my safety. His words were not about control, but about minimizing risk. I apologized. He accepted. I got it. I thanked him. He smiled. We shook hands. The incident ended.

That night, danger again sought me out, and I hoped my response was smarter than a few hours earlier. The incident began harmlessly enough as I woke from a sound sleep, needing to urinate. Leaving my tent, I beheld another majestic sky, starlight sparkles abounding in God's firmament. Yahweh Tsebaoth in Hebrew translates to "Lord of hosts," referring to the night-time stars and their creator. "Heavenly host" and "Starry host" and "King of Hosts" were other phrases I associated from scripture with this extraordinary Hebrew name for God, and this sight before me. The beauty amid tranquility and silence were something to appreciate.

Finishing my business, I felt awestruck as I beheld the night sky once more, and the waning moon. As I moved toward my tent, the stillness was broken. I heard sounds like a plastic garbage can full of trash being turned over by an animal. Such sounds I'd heard at home and it seemed familiar. I was going to let it go, thinking it insignificant—maybe just crew members.

As I parted the flap on my tent to enter, I then heard a shout, followed by a tussle, like the sides of a tent being pushed against. Then I hear a second yell and more tent-like tussling sounds. Was someone under attack by an animal? Should I jump into my tent, or try and help? (Remember "duty of care" that I learned at Mount Everest).

Well, someone needed help I thought, and I might be the closest person, so I hurried toward the continuing commotion. Uncertainty and dis-ease gripped me. As I walked I considered that calling in the cavalry to have numbers on my side was a good idea. "Help, I need help!" I called into the darkness as I walked toward the ruckus. There was no response. I apparently was the first, and only, responder. I called again and kept walking, getting near the tent. Just before I reached it, a crew member with a flashlight got there and went in. And then other flashlights appeared and I heard native language spoken. Seeing this somewhat orderly response, I stopped. Things seemed in hand, so I retreated toward my tent.

Suddenly from a corner of the darkness a man carrying a flashlight walked a diagonal line toward me, cutting me off before I could reach my tent. He aimed his flashlight at my face, then put the light on his face showing me he was one of our crew, the cook, I believe. I gave him a rundown on the last few minutes. He listened, watching me the entire time. He calmly said, "Go back to bed," and I obeyed, wondering what just happened—which I would find out in the morning.

Back in my tent, with my heartbeat returning to normal, I was about to fall asleep when in the next tent I heard what sounded like vomiting. I heard words I couldn't quite make out, but it sounded like Chris was sick and Yosra was caring for him. I considered getting up, but the situation seemed to be in hand. I said a prayer for all those in distress, and then followed directions: I was in my tent, in bed, and soon asleep.

Sunday, 14 June, 2009

At breakfast I learned the night-time confusion was one crew member having a bad dream that led to acting out. When another crew member tried to subdue and comfort him a fight broke out, the dreamer thinking his nightmare had come to life. Calm was restored by other crew as I approached. The story sounded plausible, with no wild predatory animals. Maybe some kind of disagreement broke out into fisticuffs. Gody knew of my response, but didn't rebuke me a second time. This was a different situation than the previous afternoon. We all have, I believe, a "duty of care" for our fellow human beings, and Gody must have agreed.

White-necked ravens, about the size of turkeys at home, were the vacuum cleaners at Kilimanjaro. They hung out around our camps, ready to grab any discarded food item. The Shira Camp had a robust population, all well-nourished, and their food patrols brought them near our tents. Minding Gody's coaching, they got no handouts from me and I watched my food stores closely. The cooking smells of breakfast drew them closer.

Morning clouds turned to sun for a moment, then back to clouds. Today would be a day of what I called in my journal, "Triumphs and Troubles." The troubles were for the most part a function of weather, the damp variety.

It rained, rained some more, and often the rain was a flat-out downpour. In Indiana we'd call this a gully-washer or toad strangler. And when the rain wasn't raining, it turned into hail or snow. This was a seven hour day on the mountain, with Gody and I constantly on the move except for a 30 minute lunch and a few brief rest breaks.

At mid-morning, in the distance, a volcanic formation known as Lava Tower appeared. As we moved slowly closer, the squat, imposing hulk of volcanic formation took on more definition and I could see its features, maybe even a route upward. We had our lunch at the foot of its six hundred feet of height. I'd asked Gody earlier if we could climb to the top. He assured me we could, if it were a dry day. This day was anything but dry.

In our approach to Lava Tower, first we got snowed on, then hailed on. Then rainfall resumed, making for a wet lunch. We had nothing for shelter but the parkas we wore, which were inadequate. When did I last—if ever—eat lunch in the rain, I wondered? Oh, well. I wasn't complaining or whining. I was just wet. We had cold fried chicken, a hardboiled egg, and an apple. After a prayer, I ate a few bites of each. My appetite was light due to elevation, plus a developing headache. And I felt cold.

An ascent of a soaked Lava Tower wasn't to be and Gody and I said our farewell to it, as we'd return by another route. We were in high alpine desert terrain for much of this day. Our elevation gain produced the familiar headache. Not crushing, but I clearly felt pressure and pain around my temples. Now it was tolerable; later it would cause more trouble.

Conditions became slick from the rain, snow, and hail that produced tricky footing. Then we walked across a knee-pounding streambed of boulders and shallow flowing water that left me with a lot of soreness. I became even wetter, along with being colder.

As the rain continued, we began to descend toward a spectacular feature a couple miles ahead: the Garden of Senecio and Lobelia. Footing graduated from tricky to treacherous in many spots, from glacial-melt ankle-deep stream crossings to climbing through damp, slick rocks. Gody's steady hand and strong arms helped smooth my way. The rain continued and Gody and I pressed ahead, step after step, minute after minute, for what seemed longer than a couple of miles. Soon signs of the next camp began to show. There were no actual signposts, but rather botanical evidence of the garden, and the camp was just beyond.

Our excruciating seven hour day on the mountain was reaching what should have been a fantastic close. The final descent took us into a picturesque valley that reminded me of Jurassic Park, with oversized botanical displays in the Garden of Senecio and Lobelia—a visual highlight of the trip with its own version of damp beauty.

Rainfall and accompanying mist and fog muted the views, plus I was cold, wet, and uncomfortable. Yet, I delighted in what I could see of the odd looking plants. Gody was my botanist in residence. I teased him that he hadn't warned me to expect such wonders. The groundsels resembled cactus, with blooms sprouting from their tops. Some were 150 years old I believe Gody said. They weren't much taller than me. The lobelia reminded me of huge pineapples, about half my 5'7" height. These plants are native to Kilimanjaro and its rich volcanic soil. The daytime heat of being located at the equator, and the nighttime cold of the elevation and glaciers contributed to their uniqueness.

Our new camp, a quarter-mile away, was called Barranco. Here an unwelcome visitor arrived and, expected friends did not arrive.

Unwelcome was my intense headache; unseen were my expedition friends. My anticipated reunion with my partners didn't happen, because they were rerouted to another camp. I groaned from disappointment at my headache and not being with friends.

The headache graduated to a throbbing pain and I experienced some disorientation while doing simple tent organizational tasks. All the clothes on my body were soaked, as was my gear. After much unpacking and a sorting effort that accomplished little, I lay down to nap. I missed being with Martin and Josh at The Ritz. My last view of Chris and Yosra was on the trail, where Chris was vomiting—again. I offered him some meds I had with me, but he declined. I mentioned the meds to Yosra in case Chris changed his mind. I truly missed my new friends that evening. Darn. I snacked and downed Ibuprofen and aspirin for the headache. That, plus a few winks of sleep gave me some relief. When I awakened, the rain continued and my muscles ached.

Feeling groggy I reminded myself that today was an outworking of the lesson: "Climb high—sleep low." We'd gone up to nearly 15,000 feet of elevation, and then walked down a long way, how far I didn't know. I hoped the lower elevation would revive me.

When Godlisten stopped by to visit me I was candid about how I felt. "Papa Walter," Gody asked, "Are you satisfied?"

I responded, "Yes. Today has been a day of triumph and troubles."

He accepted this without asking more. Later, I wondered what exactly he meant by the question. And what about my response? What about being called Papa Walter, as he and the other climbers now always addressed me? How did I feel about that name?

I hoped he didn't think I was finished going up, that my climb had come to an end and I felt "satisfied" by coming only this far. Had I adequately answered him, I wondered? I should have fleshed out my answer with more detail. I should have asked what he meant. Alas, I was still a little sketchy in my thinking, what with the headache and disorientation.

I came to learn my new name of "Papa" was an unexpected gift. "Papa" was a term of endearment, like being called Grandfather. Clearly I was the oldest guy in our little community. For that matter, I was probably the oldest guy on the mountain. I sure hadn't seen anyone else with a head full of gray hair, or heard reports of anyone else being 60 plus years old. I came to love the name I had first questioned as I learned its Tanazanian heritage. On returning home I encouraged my granddaughter Siena to call me Papa Walter. Years later after my climb in Argentina where my guide and friend Pete named me "Waltero" I amended it to Papa Waltero.

Godlisten took my wet clothes, a large pile, and said he'd return them the next morning—dry. How he planned to accomplish this I didn't ask, but switching out of them felt good. After supper, although still alone, I felt a little better physically. However, the steady rain continued and fog now covered the mountain instead of mist.

Nonetheless, I found room for gratitude. "Ahsante. Ahsante sana." That translates from Swahili to "Thank you. Thank you very much." I said it to God Almighty. My head felt a little better, I had dry clothes, I had eaten food, drank hot tea and water, and was ready for bed. Some day!

But I still missed my friends—it felt disheartening not to have them camping next to me, because we'd formed a delightful community. I hoped Chris felt better and looked forward to a possible reunion the next day. In my confusion, I hadn't asked Gody about them. Dumb.

I also missed my family and being home. With that, alone in my tent and feeling lonely, I slipped into my sleeping bag.

Monday, 15 June, 2009

I slept fairly well as my headache eased. *Thank you, God.* And the niggles disappeared—*thanks again.* Overnight while on my customary nature outing to drain my bladder, I noted the sky was clearing and I could see Kibo, the Shining Mountain, closer than ever. I felt such gratitude for being there, for seeing the mountain, for my body, mind, and spirit. I remembered how the mountain guides would say "one per cent of the population get to climb mountains." How blessed was I.

Brrrr—the temperature dropped overnight, but my sleeping bag stayed warm. I was grateful for it also, and for the sun that greeted me as I emerged from my tent.

I made delightful discoveries that morning. I begin sharing sticks of chewing gum with the crew, who loved it. And, then, lo and behold, my trek mates—Martin and Josh, and Chris and Yosra, were in my very camp! More thanks! In the downpour of heavy rain, the ground fog, and the scurry to get settled, I simply didn't see them arrive, nor did they see me.

The gum sharing became a morning delight. I'd brought a lot of chewing gum along for myself and soon realized I had more than I needed. I hope I am a giving person, both of things and of myself. Sharing gum with the crew was instinctive, and I did so each morning. The practice began there at the Garden as I went on a camp walkabout, seeking out all of the crew for the three teams, guides, porters, cooks to give each man (there were no women in the support crew) a stick. This first day began the distribution of Papa Walter's gum.

Inadvertently, I overlooked one of the porters who found me a few minutes later, with a hang-dog look on his face and one word on his lips, "Gum." Realizing the problem, I apologized, reached into my pocket, and gave him a piece of gum. His broad smile matched mine. A new tradition had begun.

Thinking about the day before, I realized the fog and mist were thick, both in the garden area and inside my head from the headache and disorientation. That's why I thought my new friends, my fellow climbers, were re-routed elsewhere. I had asked one of the crew, although not Godlisten, about them and perhaps he misunderstood my question. His answer led me to believe they were over-nighting elsewhere.

Anyhow, Martin and Josh had their tent near mine, with Chris and Yosra not far from them. Martin saw me and called out, "Walter!" Like that, we re-knitted back together again.

If the previous day was Triumph and Troubles, then this day was titled Challenge and Triumph. My UK mates called our trekking and climbing efforts "scrambling." And we scrambled much of the day. My word for some of the spots we found ourselves in: treacherous. We even did rock climbing, something I had not trained for. Perhaps I overstate the challenge, but that's how it seemed like to me.

During much of the morning I felt keenly aware of a single reason I steadily advanced upward: Godlisten's strength, his hand clasping mine, and his calm sureness as he pulled me up, through, and over tight spots. We climbed a tough section of rock which hundreds of thousands of years ago was hot, dripping lava from Kibo's eruption. The rock sections were 10 and 20 feet in height and went nearly straight up. When I struggled, Gody would go first, plant himself, and then grasp my outstretched hand and pull me straight up— hauling my weight of 160-ish pounds, plus a backpack weighing 25 pounds. One strong dude was above me: Godlisten. My trek boots would find footholds, he pulled, and up went Papa Walter. After several false summits, areas I was lulled into thinking were the top of the difficult section of "scrambling" up these lava pitches, we finally found ourselves above this arduous area. Wow! What a view!

A rest break was in order at this point, from where we had a clear view of the southern ice fields—glacial ice deposits of the Heim, Kersten, and Decken glaciers. Yesterday's route was visible far in the distance, along with waterfalls at the garden. Knowing we wouldn't return this way, I tried to memorize the beauty and photograph it. Ahead, glacial ice overlaying the mountain reminded me of frosting on a Bundt cake dripping down the baked sides.

We were now back on the trail itself, but in a picturesque place to view the upper mountain. Scrambling over for now, we resumed trekking, as we had more miles to cover before reaching our campsite. So we trekked on, one foot in front of the other. This day was five hours of up, up, and more up before finally reaching the Karanga Valley campsite. The name was a little deceiving because we were atop the valley, not within it. This was known as the last place to gather water before our push to the summit

On that night, our little mountain community, including Chris and Yosra, regathered in Martin and Josh's Ritz tent for a lovely dinner to crown a challenging day.

The fog disruption that kept us all in our own tents the previous night had confused our "wait staff," who wondered if they'd done something wrong because we all ate in our individual tents. They said something in Swahili I didn't understand, but their facial cues suggested they were bewildered. We assured them we appreciated their kindnesses and we liked getting together. They may not have understood our words, but they could see the happiness in our faces and the laughter coming from The Ritz as the five of us talked about everything.

Over dinner, I told my friends how much I missed my family. They commiserated. Martin and Josh and Chris and Yosra discussed getting together when they returned to London, each noting some curry specialty houses they knew. Yosra spoke of their recent wedding in her Egyptian homeland and what was involved. They had thought Kili would be a fun change of pace as a honeymoon destination.

We also talked about the mountain's challenges during the day and I admitted feeling tested by places that seemed perilous to me, yet I was enjoying the experience. Godlisten proved extremely helpful to me, but my friends didn't necessarily see that kind of outreach from their guides. Perhaps because they were so much younger, the other guides didn't consider offering extra help. Everyone agreed Godlisten was a special person and I was fortunate to have him.

Chris wondered if he'd make the summit. He nodded toward Yosra and said, "She's the strong one, stronger than me. She can do it."

Martin and Josh were two of the most laid back characters I would meet on any mountain. They were upbeat and seemed to take everything in their stride. Yes, they exhibited some of the sarcasm and condescension Brits are known for, but they verbally played in a light, funny way, never mean-spirited. The three of us had tennis in common and talked about it most days. I settled into a kind of peer, yet senior, role by virtue of my age, plus having been to Everest Base Camp. By this time I happily answered to just about everyone calling me Papa Walter. After all, I was older than everyone, including Gody, perhaps by as much as 20 years.

At least I wasn't slowing the group, and staying close on the heels of guys and a gal younger than Dominic and Andrew made me happy.

As the conversation ranged around the table, with all of us having something to say and everyone else willing to listen, I mused that this was authentic camaraderie, rare and precious. But all of us felt a little weathered from the day and we soon headed off to sleeping bags in our own tents.

Tuesday, 16 June, 2009

An awesome sunrise graced the mountain. One byproduct of this sunny dawn was the miles-long shadow cast by Kilimanjaro. From our point of view the sun arced upward from behind the mountain, thus creating the silhouette we saw before us—the most expansive shadow I'd ever seen, miles wide and even more miles long, bathing the entire Karanga Valley in the mountain's shadow outline.

Today's climb would be our big day before the biggest day tomorrow. We ascended to Barafu ("ice" in Swahili) Camp which put us above 15,000 feet in elevation. This staging set us up for summit day, which would actually begin at night, before midnight, when we'd be awakened at 11 p.m.

As we made our way around the mountain climbing toward Barafu, the Southern Ice Fields appeared on our left and we saw the Rebmann Glacier for the first time. I was interested to learn the glaciers often carried the name of missionaries. Glaciers named for missionaries—what was up with that?

The first mountaineers on Kilimanjaro were Christian missionaries who came to East Africa for two reasons: To claim it for Christ, as Christian missionaries do, by converting the natives. Second, and equally important, they wished to terminate the slave trade that originated here. Many American slaves of the Civil War era and before could trace their ancestral origins to East Africa. I remembered the classic Christian song "Amazing Grace" was written by a ship captain whose vessel carried slaves bound from East Africa.

While in country, many of the missionaries were fascinated by Kilimanjaro. Snow on a mountain at the equator seemed preposterous. One Englishman scholar scoffed at the idea for decades in his writings. Remarkably, he did this from his desk without ever traveling to Africa. Prideful. He ruined people's reputations by ridiculing their visions of snow on an equatorial mountain. Ultimately, science and truth won out and the humiliation he heaped on others turned back on him. European and English missionaries happened to be among the first Westerners to see the mountain with its snow and glaciers, and then climb it.

Now, hanging in my kitchen at home is a picture of the southern ice fields on the flanks of Kilimanjaro, with me in the foreground on a rest break. Godlisten shot the photo on our last stop before reaching Barafu. In the pic, I wear a hat from Everest, made of yak wool, one of the warmest natural fabrics known to man.

Vegetation was sparse as we are neared the elevation where plants could no longer grow in the thin air. The temperatures were cold during the daytime now. My yak hat felt warm on my head and when I sipped my water-lemon-lime Gatorade mix through the plastic hose connected to a bladder located in my pack, the liquid tasted cold from the change in temperature due to the increased elevation. I was staying hydrated, had acclimatized, and was breathing appropriately for this elevation—okay, but not like at sea level. And certainly better than I would breathe at 4,000 feet higher tomorrow! The trek boots I'd worn to Everest Base Camp felt comfortable and my feet stayed warm within them. My feet and boots were doing yeoman work.

Our climbing day neared a close as we rounded the mountain, putting the ice field behind our left shoulders. We'd see it again tomorrow along with other glaciers—up close and personal.

After completing the day's ascent to Barafu we signed in at the ranger's national park hut, a small, circular metal enclosure that seemed ordinary from the outside. Inside, I was amazed to see Coca Cola, Kilimanjaro Beer, another kind of beer, and T-shirts for sale. At 15,358 feet of elevation, this was high altitude merchandising for sure. I knew every item for sale had to be trekked in, because choppers seldom flew around Kili—and certainly not to deliver merchandise. I couldn't imagine what those beverages would do to my system, nor did I care to find out. Water with Gatorade was what I needed and wanted—pronto. I was still meeting my goal of three liters a day, and that regime helped me avoid the worst altitude symptoms. I had a little headache and fatigue, but that was to be expected. Thankfully, though I felt dizziness, my thinking seemed ordered—at least as clear as it ever got.

At this campsite the porters set up our three sleeping tents close together, because level ground was limited and the campsite overflowed with climbers who, in the Apostle Paul's words for salvation, "had their eye on the prize." Not that our destination (Uhuru Peak) was Heaven, but it was Africa's highest point. In my theologian's mind, Heaven is above us. Thus, mountains are as close as we can get to Heaven while our feet still touch the soil of Earth. So, here in Africa, tomorrow at sunrise at 19,340 feet—God willing—we would be as close as we could get to the prize.

After caching our gear in our tents, the five of us, Josh, Martin, Yosra, Chris, and I, hung out together, took photos, stayed warmed, and rested. We snapped pics of each other and asked another climber to take shots of the five of us, using our individual cameras. We had truly bonded.

We arrived in mid-afternoon and each of us needed to prepare our gear for the next day before an early supper. I didn't wish to leave the good company, but I am meticulous around gear preparation, and knew this would take time. We all planned to rendezvous at the Ritz for early dining.

Inside my tent, while preparing for the awesome adventure ahead, I felt somewhat breathless while moving about, for good reason. The elevation of 15,000 feet will do that. I was in awe of what lay ahead of, and above us. I had climbed to 17,600 feet of elevation at Everest Base Camp, but Uhuru Peak was 2,000 feet higher.

"I have what it takes," I told myself. Then, I revised my thinking. "Hold on ego. That was a rash statement—that immodesty needs amending. What I should have said was: I have done my best to prepare for Shining Mountain. This is no place for vanity or ego. With self-assurance I wish, I hope, to do my best. I believe with courage and hope, I may make it to Uhuru Peak." I said this respectfully, minus bravado.

The mountain would decide who reached her summit, not me. However, I knew I should also believe in myself. To dismissively sell myself short would be an indication that I didn't belong there.

I concluded: "Dear God, help me do my best. I so wish to make it. To believe in myself is not immodest. To believe in me is to have courage. You expected that of Joshua in Chapter One in his book of the Bible, right? The word 'courage' comes up there what, four times in your direction and counsel to Joshua, right? May I have courage also. Courage, I believe, strengthens hope. May it be so, God, you who created this mountain."

As I began to organize and pack, I paused once more and told myself, "This is for much more than me. This is also for the children who will go through the clinical program; for the clinicians who will help them; and for our donors. Bless them all, won't you, God?"

I spread out seven layers of clothes for my upper body and four layers for waist and below. I mixed three liters of water with Gatorade. I had several hot pack inserts. Knowing the summit temperature would be well below freezing, I duct taped some of the hot packs to my bladder with hose and water bottles to (hopefully) keep them from freezing. I put out extra hand warmers for my down parka pockets where I would store my St. Vincent

Blackberry and my camera to keep their batteries warm. I selected more warmers for the chest area pockets to keep my upper body warm, and two more for my gloves. I carried spares in case I or someone else needed them, or if I found a defective pack.

Headlamp out: Check.

Trek poles: Check.

Ski goggles: Check.

Backup gloves: Check.

Mini-Bible out for my attention first thing after I wake up: Check.

And so on down the punch list. Check ... Check ... Check....

When I had my gear in place, it occupied about half of the tent. Geez, I wondered how the other crew members managed with a second person in the tent.

Our "reservations" at the Ritz were for 4:30 and I arrived a few minutes early, bringing extra hand warmer packs to see if anyone needed them. Martin and Josh had the table and chairs ready. The porters, I noticed, had stopped setting up the extra dining tents, which saved them time and also spoke to the fact that the five of us had bonded so well we only needed a single tent. Here at Barafu, where space for tents was at a premium, our economizing helped other expeditions.

Yosra and Chris arrived, and soon the waiters brought hot water for tea and began ferrying food to the table. I asked my four friends if I might say a prayer, as in a few hours our huge summit day would commence. I hoped to bless all of us in advance, along with the food. Everyone agreed.

I prayed aloud in thanksgiving for our bodies, minds, and spirits, and for the safety we experienced in reaching Barafu. I asked God's blessings on our summit day, for favorable weather, for summit success, and for continued safety. I asked a blessing on each and all of us, and for our families and the crew. And a blessing on the food, of course. I "amened" it and everyone thanked me.

Before our food arrived, Gody dropped by the tent to give his final instructions as lead guide for the entire expedition. He was in great spirits, and somehow or other ended up serenading us with a song in Swahili with a refrain concerning "No worries." He sang loudly, with great enthusiasm. His joy was infectious.

Yet, our up-beatness had a somber side. During our meal we grew a little quiet at times. We all knew we would rise at 11 p.m., get dressed, have a little something to eat and drink, visit the loo, and be off before midnight. I hoped and planned to reach the summit in time for sunrise around 6:15 a.m. I had communicated this to Gody and it was doable, he said.

All five of us knew our summit day was a serious undertaking and Kilimanjaro had a high washout rate of about fifty percent. That's a huge rate of un-success. Moreover, some park authorities spoke of two climbing deaths per year, while others placed the total as high as ten deaths a year. In fact, one death would happen during our climb. Injuries and illness were common.

We had good reasons for concern. Tomorrow we would climb from 15,000 feet to above 19,000 feet and then descend about 10,000 feet—a long, challenging day during which the temperature would be -4 below zero F before sunrise. At the end of our day the temp would be at 40 degrees F – a wide swing of 44 degrees. We had trekked through the rain forest, heather, and moorland. Barafu, our present location, was in the high alpine desert zone. Within a few hours we'd move into the arctic weather zone.

I felt good. I felt prepared, respectfully confident, and a bit cautious. So much could go wrong on a mountain. And on Kilimanjaro, at 19,340 feet, I would be well above my Everest personal record of 17,600. The elevations and my response reminded me of what Fr. Adrian VanKaam, one of my mentors, called "a pace of grace."

Twenty five months earlier, the elevation I reached at Everest had been below my aspirations. I hoped for 18,200 by summiting Kala Patar, a lesser peak in Everest's long shadow, but still higher than Everest Base Camp. That was not to be, however. Acute mountain sickness and other issues thwarted my plans. As a competitive and driven person, I was disappointed. Thanks to maturity born of grace, I accepted the reality and my disappointment with docility and humility.

Now, two years later, I contemplated a summit 1,100 feet higher than Kala Patar. OMG. "Pace of grace" indeed Adrian, and thanks for the teaching.

I ate what was put before us, but perhaps less than I usually consumed. Appetites can evaporate at high altitudes. Our server noticed. "Papa," he said, "you must eat." And I did eat more. They served us that stew thing again, perhaps a little spicier this time. And, of course, the blood left my brain to go to my stomach and digest the food leaving, me a little more light-headed than before.

I thought I ate too much; I hoped I ate enough. Who can tell at altitude? I appreciated the crew member urging me to eat more, but the food seemed to hang in my stomach. Since the time was only 6 p.m. I hoped it would digest before the trek began. With good wishes all round, I left the Ritz after a toast with tea and handshakes to conclude our evening. Soon I was tucked into my sleeping bag, having already layered on some of my climbing clothes. I spent a fitful, restless evening with little sleep. Rascal neighbors (not our group) next door laughed and talked at high volume. From my sleeping bag, I voiced protestations: "Shut up already!" Ultimately they did, and the night grew silent and calm then—for a while.

Then Mother Nature threw a weather tantrum that had me wondering, "What is Kilmanjaro saying to me, to us?"

We got a heavy storm with rain and wind. When this ended, snow began falling. The rain came down so hard I honestly thought someone might be throwing buckets of water against my tent. This continued on for a spell, and then the wind kicked up, strong enough that I thought about "the mighty wind" mentioned in Genesis at the beginning of the Bible. The tent fabric shook and vibrated to and fro under the strain. When the wind picked up another notch in noise and force, I wondered if my tent would sail off that pinnacle of rock called Barafu Camp, with me in it, like some misguided magic carpet.

"What is Kilimanjaro saying?" I wondered.

I don't remember if the weather tantrum stopped first, or if I fell asleep, despite it.

Wednesday, 17 June, 2009

My summit day was captured in an article I sent to Brittany Hersch Keener, my associate at St. Vincent Jennings in North Vernon. Britt prepared and distributed a blog we used to report on the climb and fuel interest in the youth weight management program being started at St. Vincent Jennings. Our dual aim was to raise awareness about youth obesity and what St. Vincent Jennings could do to prevent and treat it, and to raise money for funding the clinic and offering scholarships to low income patients. Thanks to Brittany for producing and distributing all the blogs. This account was written in the freshness and afterglow of the summit moment and is an apt portrayal of my Kili summit day.

Our team had spent five days climbing Mount Kilimanjaro, moving into position for an early morning try for the summit of Uhuru Peak. For perspective, the elevation of the village of Moshi, where we began, was 5,000+ feet, a little higher than Denver. We were now on the final leg, heading more than 4,000 feet into the thin air to reach 19,340 feet, the roof of Africa.

We would purposefully put one foot in front of the other in a kind of controlled slow-motion to try and ward off altitude sickness. We had already climbed through the damp, muddy (and hot and humid) rain forest, into gathering clouds nicknamed the cloud forest, upward into the heath and grassy moorland. We then crossed up into the alpine desert.

And now on summit night, we would, God willing, ascend through the nighttime darkness to the glacial ice cap. While climbing the world's tallest free-standing mountain, Kilimanjaro, the peak seemed near Heaven.

I switched on my flashlight at Gody's 11 p.m. wake up call. Having all my clothes out in advance helped me avoid being a truant school boy on this important day. Off to the loo and thankful to be void, I pulled on seven upper layers and four trouser layers of clothes. I put hand warmers in my gloves, and in my pockets where I had cameras to keep their batteries warm. I even taped hand warmers to my water supply.

I joked that I left a yellow urine stream up and down Kili, because I worked hard to avoid under-hydrating as I had at Everest. The Diamox (altitude medication) was working, and I took Ibuprofen as needed for muscle aches. Bengay was my topical soreness reliever—and its smell opened my sinuses. As I had no opportunities to bathe, Bengay became my Hoosier cologne. I also carried Dexamethazone, a steroid, in case I suffered the debilitating acute mountain sickness I experienced while trekking to Mount Everest Base Camp 25 months earlier.

I noticed my Go-Zone pedometer from Virgin Health Miles must have taken a hit as I scrambled up boulders. Somewhere along the way it stopped working. I was walking 66 linear miles and was keen on what data my VHM Go-Zone pedometer would disclose. Alas, it must've banged against a rock and stopped working. Later I discovered it was functioning fine, but the memory had maxed out. It took a beating and had kept on ticking—way to go you Go-Zone engineers!

I flew my "colors" proudly that day. Everyone on the mountain seemed to notice the large color poster on my backpack proclaiming Trek for Kids for Pediatric Obesity for St. Vincent Jennings Hospital. Many, many people complimented the idea. A pretty lass from Paris, with some help from me, made, the connection between the historical Vincent de Paul's ministry based in Paris and our hospital. "Oh, they must be so very proud of you there," she said.

Godlisten was physically strong, emotionally calm, and vigilant for my safety, proving a commendable match for me. In humility and honesty, let me be clear: I could not have climbed the 15,000 feet to Barafu without his help. In a similar manner, he made the difference on our summit night, so I climbed well. He coached, encouraged, and guided me at every turn. The Whiskey Route up Machame lived up to its name for toughness, length, steepness, and beauty when compared to the more mundane routes (as if anything on Kili may be called a mundane!).

We had spent our summit-eve high on Barafu in Kili's rarefied air of 15,000 feet elevation where the oxygen was in short supply. It was like breathing through a straw. What would 4,000 feet higher be like, I mused?

The porters would awaite our return to Barafu Camp because we would take an out-back turn-around route to Uhuru Peak. I marveled at the four porters who ferried tents, cooking gear, expedition bags, food and whatever else by balancing the gear on their heads while customarily walking faster than my more snailish pace. What strength, what balance ... loads always faithfully packed safely from one camp to the next. We greeted each other happily with "Jambo" meaning "Good morning" or "Hello." My cook had the most pleasant smile and wanted so to please ... as an example, serving eggs for breakfast with hot dogs for sausage, fresh pineapple, mango, avocado, and pancakes that were more like crepes (and went well with Red Gold brand preserves).

(A dinner discovery I made was that Elwood, Indiana based Red Gold products were on our camp table. When I later told this to a friend at St. Vincent Mercy Hospital in Elwood, Angie said, "I knew I was with you in spirit, I just didn't know I was in your ketchup!") We also had porridge and hot water for powdered drinks, cocoa for me, while all my UK-based friends enjoyed their customary tea. The cooking was generally hot, fresh, and good. I hated to disappoint my cook on days when the high elevation stole my appetite. "You must eat Papa," was his lament and kindly advice.

I had some appropriate shoulder soreness from the pack straps, but nary a blister on my feet. Sometimes breathless, I felt the dull throb of an altitude headache and it seemed everyone spoke of this also. I had no niggles or diarrhea, thankfully. Thankfully, no edema problems affecting my balance. I was still thinking clearly—well, as clearly as one could think at 15,000 feet. Except for last night, I still slept fairly well, although my inner alarm stayed on Indiana time and awakened me at 5 a.m.—eight hours earlier than in Tanzania.

"Digala, Digala," Gody's voice boomed as we set off toward the summit. The loose Swahili translation of this was "Superduper." Our head lamps lighted the pathway ahead and the stormy wind, rain, and snow of overnight was gone. As we set off to climb, the Creator God beamed a night sky vast and filled with gleaming stars. A sliver of moon joined the festivities – sitting in the sky as though a saucer, a lunar look I wasn't familiar with. And no wind. "Thank you, God for the weather." This reminded me of the story when Jesus becalmed a storm with a two word instruction, "Be calm."

Gody led the way as we climbed across—and up—slick, snow-covered lava boulders on the switchback scree, the dark pierced by the narrow beam of our lamps. We went straight up at first, and one miscue here would lead to a dangerous fall. I trusted Gody without question, marveling at how he found the route with only a headlamp. "When you've climbed Kili 150 times in 15 years, you have the map up here," he said while pointing an index finger to his head. We climbed. We drank. We climbed. I stopped making the demoralizing mistake of looking up the mountain to see the headlights above us. Seeing a few climbers above only reminded me of what was ahead. Knowing was enough—I didn't need to see how far and how steep the terrain would be from here to there, and beyond. My glasses fogged up, so I took them off and pulled down my ski goggles. I was feeling strong, but knew we were only at the midpoint of a huge ordeal.

Up we continued. I focused my vision on Gody's boots in front of me, placing my own boots in his footsteps. With my leader striding ahead I found a rhythm, a comfortable and deliberate pace. The temperature felt bitter cold, despite my layers of clothing. I gave thanks for all the swaddling clothing I wrapped myself within, even though I resembled the Michelin Tire Man. I truly needed those hand-warmers for my fingers, and to keep the batteries of my cameras juiced. But so much for my engineering ingenuity with the hand warmers on my water supply as, when I tried to drink, the tube had gelled with ice. Oops.

The only sounds were our footfalls on the trail of dried volcanic scree from eons past, and our labored breathing in the thin air. I was comfortable with silence. Those footfalls and breathing became my melodies. Was that my heartbeat I heard also?

About 2 a.m. I needed a boost. Remembering Gody's singing, I asked him to do so believing that would revive my spirit and give me something to hear other than my boot steps and breathing. He sang the song about "No Worries." It was so good I wanted more. I then "called in" a request - a song I'd heard him sing, a Christian favorite: "What a Friend We Have in Jesus."

A timeless mountain moment followed.

Gody began singing in Swahili in his customary enthusiastic and loud way, bringing a smile to my face. A few second later, from way up the mountain the guides in front of us heard the singing and picked up the refrain. Meanwhile, the many guides behind joined in as well. Talk about one spirit's soaring. Music is such a universal language. The singing went on for five minutes and more it seemed. Gregorian chanting at my seminary at Meinrad, as beautiful as it was, never sounded this good. As Julie Andrews sang in "The Sound of Music," borrowing a line from the psalmist, "The hills" (well, mountains) "are alive with the sound of music." Later, I heard climbers I didn't know speak of the moment, referring to "community singing on the mountain in the dark." I wasn't trying for an evangelical moment, but, oh, my goodness.

Gody brought us to a halt to check his watch. "Uh, oh," he said in his shorthand English, "We are way ahead of schedule. Papa Walter you are strong climber. Simba, like lion. We will get there early. You climb very good, not just for 61 man (my age), but for anyone. You are now Papa Walter Simba." Gody thereby bolstered the term of affection with which he'd christened me.

"Thank you, God for body, mind, and spirit, and for training." Papa Walter Simba, my new name. Thank you, Gody.

We summited Kilimanjaro's Uhuru Peak at 0610 on 17 June, minutes before a majestic sunrise. We were surrounded by the panoramic beauty and palette of the Creator God Elohim's world:

Gigantic chalky colored glaciers soared as far as the eye could see to my right. The volcanic crater of Kilimanjaro from which the megatons of lava erupted centuries ago, now saucered in an almost perfect circle, dormant below the Roof of Africa, hosting even more frozen glaciers as sentinels nearby. A glorious red and gold sunrise crept over the horizon as it rose above the white billowy Cloud Forest thousands of feet below us. Cobalt blue skies pushed away the navy blue darkness above.

The play of equatorial sunlight on God's nature made me wonder how our beautiful Beatitudes stained glass windows at the St. Vincent Jennings Hospital Chapel would have looked in this celestial light.

Suddenly Gody gave me a huge hug, lifted me off my feet, and hoisted me into the air while laughing and congratulating me. With his lift I laughed and told him I was three feet higher than the summit—19,343 feet! We laughed and hugged each other.

The up-mountain journey required six hours and ten minutes from when we left camp at midnight.

We took pictures of the two of us with arms around each other, framed by the historic Kilimanjaro sign of welcome and place, as a faint red sunrise glow edged into the photo. Of all the pictures I have from all the mountains, this remains one of my favorites.

I carried a mallard duck feather given me by my Indiana University college friend Mark Fritz, who asked me to release the feather from the summit in a ritual to remember IU college friends of 40+ years. I did this while offering prayers for us, our families, and those who had died, including Mark's son. I prayed also for the young people who would be involved in our obesity prevention and treatment program, for their clinicians, and for program sponsors and donors. I prayed for Wings for the Journey parents who lost beloved children, and I said their children's names. I remembered the names of my own family members who had died and told them, "I love you, I miss you, and thank you." And I thought about my sons Dom and Andy and their families. I felt a little emotional after all that.

My water line that had jelled on the way up had a surprise awaiting my thirst. When I sucked on the spigot I noticed the line had thawed and water was flowing. It got me laughing to think all the body warmth from being excited had thawed the line.

Gody had agreed to my requests to trek into the crater so I could touch a glacier. I told him I might kiss the glacier! However, I called off those plans, knowing it would add even more hours to the daylong descent that awaited us. I could have stayed up top longer, but it was time to begin our descent. And so we started down.

"Hold on, Gody, I need to gather stones for souvenirs." S-m-a-l-l stones ... weight considerations.

WHAT GOES UP

I made the right decision about not taking extra hours to trek to the volcano crater and kiss a glacier. Because you see, what goes up ... must come down, knackered knees and legs and all.

As strong as Gody believed I was on the way up, I had used a great deal of energy in the ascent. Traveling down-mountain, we walked across BB sized and marble-like scree. I couldn't keep my balance and bearings in the downhill, switchback trail of snow, sand and scree. As strong as I felt going up, my knees and legs were knackered on the way down trying to negotiate what seemed like a ski slope. Gody was invaluable in getting me down the slippery slope. Arm-in-arm, two children of God, a Tanzanian and a Hoosier, ebony and ivory, one weak and the other strong, a Lutheran and a Catholic, he was the shepherd, me the sheep.

When finally we crossed the land bridge separating a chasm on either side and got back into Barafu camp, all I wanted to do was roll into my tent, rest my weary legs, and sleep. Ah, but after a short nap and lunch, we had another three hour trek to reach the next camp. That descent became four to five hours in my eroded and depleted weakness. We arrived at the camp in late afternoon.

What a day—what a night and day—from 12 midnight to 5 p.m. The thermometer was minus 4 below zero at the summit, and 44 degrees when we reached camp. We descended 10,000 feet from the glacial ice on the Roof of Africa, down through the alpine desert, down further to the grassy moorland and finally into the rain forest. At last I lay flat on the ground in my tent and atop my sleeping bag, breathing dense, oxygen-rich air. Thank you, God, oh, so much.

The wash-out rate of fifty percent of climbers falling short of Uhuru Peak did not quite hold true for our group. The newlyweds failed to summit. Martin and Josh, the Brits, reached the top, as did I. So our tiny community exceeded the 50 per cent summit wash-out rate for our wonderful little mobile mountain cosmopolitan village.

Chris and Josra were leaving our Barafu Camp as I came down and, sadly, I didn't get to wish them farewell. Martin and Josh were nearing the summit as I began my descent—I knew the peak was in the bag for them. We were back at the Ritz later in the evening.

Enduring friendships resulted from my time on Kilimanjaro. Martin and I occasionally exchanged emails after our return home. And with Godlisten, one of the most wonderful people I have ever known, I still exchange regular emails and gifts at Christmas.

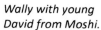
Wally with young David from Moshi.

Godlisten, Walter's guide and friend.

The wonderful crew with Godlisten center left, and Papa Walter Simba on his right.

Expedition Colleagues: Front from left, Chris and Yosra;
Back: Walter, Josh and Martin.

The crew at work transporting gear.
This was their customary way of carrying.

Foggy garden in the Barranco Valley.

Godlisten, Walter's guide and friend.

One of the glaciers near Uhuru Peak, the summit of Kilimanjaro.

Perspective and Memoriam

*M*y summit came 120 years after the first person summited Mount Kilimanjaro in October 1889. As fulfilling as this ascent of Kilimanjaro was for me and others, it is important to place this trek and summiting in perspective. During our week on Kilimanjaro, a 22 year old man trekking with his mother became ill on Kili from altitude sickness. He sought emergency room care at the hospital in Moshi, my village. I was told by someone at the emergency room and familiar with the circumstances that the young man died in the hospital. I am a hospital chaplain and much of the holy ground on which I walk often involves being with parents who've lost children. I still say prayers for this man's mother and family. In pursuit of adventure, something went tragically wrong and life changed forever for a family. May the Master Comforter provide mercy, peace, faith, grace, and, ultimately, hope.

Then, a week after returning home, I learned of an Indiana physician who climbed Kilimanjaro with his wife the summer before I. While I climbed Kili, the doctor and his wife were in Nepal on the same trek I had taken to Mount Everest Base Camp. The doctor, age 61, was from Bloomington, (a nearby community

I know well and where I lived as an undergrad student at Indiana University) and had just died in Nepal after suffering pulmonary and cerebral edema at Everest Base Camp. I experienced the beginnings of cerebral edema at Everest Base Camp. As I came home, the physician's widow began mourning her loss in a land half a world away from home. I still pray for her.

I know mountains, including Kilimanjaro, and especially Everest, claim lives. Because of parallel processes involving connections and timing, the two most recent deaths on Kilimanjaro and Everest caused me to grieve. Those two mountains I knew well had claimed two more lives. And as I have continued to climb, mountains claimed more lives. Meantime, I breathe, I live. Life, however, has changed for that mother and that wife, without their permission. Join me in a prayer for them, won't you?

At Kilimanjaro in my gear I carried three-inch purple crocheted crosses given to me by Margaret of our St. Vincent Jennings Hospital Guild to carry on Kili. An ardent Christian, Margaret crafted the crosses for youth groups, church missionaries, and just to hand out. "They remind of Jesus," Margaret said. As we visited one day at the gift shop desk, I saw she was making them and asked if I might have one to take with me to Kilimanjaro. Margaret happily complied and gave me three crosses—one which she now has, one she gave to me, and the third she presented, via me, to my beautiful grand-daughter Siena Grace Glover for the occasion of her baptism.

I took three extra vacation days, after 48 long hours, to travel home from Africa before returning to St. Vincent Jennings. I wanted this time to percolate, process, relive and store memories, and absorb the trek without talking about it. Of course I discussed the trip with my loved ones—sons Dom and Andy. But before going public, I wanted to silently treasure the memories in my heart, as is said of Mary and others (Hannah, Ruth, Esther) in the Bible after their transcendental moments. Giving voice to recollections too early would diminish them, it seemed to me. And, having trained as a journalist, I have a bias to compose with words and record things at the keyboard—to handwrite and journal first-blush sentences before speaking. And, I believe it's bad form to talk about the next step without fully appreciating the present moments, absorbing what was accomplished, and being receptive to the blessings and messages we have received.

And after absorbing what I had accomplished, the logical question arose: "What's up next for me?" The authentic answer fell somewhere between the calendar and what my legs told me as I descended Kili: "Try this again and there will be a revolt. We'll go on strike." Really, my legs said that loud and clear while Gody and I took a rest break. I had dreams of future climbing, but they were for the calendar and my lower extremities to resolve.

I had to weigh the constant headache, muscle pain, nausea, lack of appetite, breathlessness, light headedness, knackered legs and knees, and tough sleeping on one side of the scale, with the other side of the scale holding euphoria at seeing the magnificence of God's created order, having my dreams fulfilled, and the strength I gained from training and peak accomplishment— the tirelessness and seemingly unlimited and inexhaustible physical energy. That's how I saw it.

Afterword

*L*and mass plates moving deep within our planet lead to continental shifts and earthquakes. Himalayan mountains like Everest resulted when India pushed under Asia—gradually, and in big earthquake-producing surges. Volcanos erupt when molten rock and gases from deep within Earth break through the surface and explode. In the East African Rift Valley, Kilimanjaro rose on the shoulders of smaller sister volcanos Meru and Shira from volcanic explosions. After my Kilimanjaro trip, it seemed the tectonic forces that create mountains had lesser force cousins at work within my soul

In addition to my soul's seismic shifts, a molten lava of passion within me coalesced into a crazy dream. I began to imagine that I—a flatlander hospital chaplain within a few years of retirement— could make a dynamic quest to climb the Seven Summits; the highest mountains on each of the seven continents. Only one thing kept this idea from appearing egotistic, manic, and delusional: an altruistic gyroscope seemed to be steering my dreams.

My dream was to climb the highest mountain on each of seven continents. The altruism indicated by my personal gyroscope suggested that each climb should raise money to fund the youth weight management clinics. The Kilimanjaro climb had raised $22,000 to begin the youth weight management clinic at St. Vincent Jennings in North Vernon. Incidentally, I paid my own expedition expenses, so all the money I raised went directly into clinic projects.

Still, I wondered: Was it reasonable to think I could climb the Seven Summits, or was I seriously deranged? I took pressure off myself by saying publicly: "Of course it's ridiculous to think I can climb the Seven Summits. I'm almost 65 years old. I couldn't possibly do them all, especially returning to Everest to summit. That's nuts, right?"

Then I'd pause, smile, and wryly observe, "Of course, the oldest fella to accomplish the Seven Summits was about 70 when he did so. And the oldest guy to climb Everest was 80 years old." I reminded myself I had successfully summited my first of the Seven Summits, having now climbed on two of the seven.

My life was changing in other ways. My hospital ministry was about to evolve because I'd been invited to migrate to the newest St. Vincent hospitals, one in Salem and the other in Bedford, my hometown. These soon became the sites of new youth weight management clinics.

While getting ready to begin my new ministries in southern Indiana, I decided to say YES to the climbing challenge. I set my quest's international compass toward the next mountain: Mount Elbrus in Russia.

However, before moving to the Salem and Bedford hospitals, I needed to complete the start-up of the Jennings youth weight management clinic. While doing so, I met Lori Walton, a registered nurse who co-founded and ran the youth obesity program at Peyton Manning Children's Hospital at St. Vincent in Indianapolis. I invited Lori to visit North Vernon to meet with their pediatric clinical staff and help guide development of the youth management program.

We began as colleagues and became good friends. Lori, an athlete in her own right, said she'd like to accompany me to Russia to climb Mt. Elbrus. We became training partners and would summit Mount Elbrus in Russia 53 weeks after I climbed Kilimanjaro. The Elbrus climb raised another $22K for the North Vernon clinic. And a second of the Seven Summits was in the bag.

When my ministry focus shifted, Lori, who dreamed of expanding youth weight management prevention and treatment to twenty-some St. Vincent hospitals, visited my new posts to help start the youth obesity clinics at Salem, then Bedford.

Another transition was also underway—a personal seismic shift as Lori and I became romantic partners. You will read more about that in the books ahead.

As the two new clinics opened, my quest for the Seven Summits continued toward a boiling point. In the following January, 2011, I climbed in Australia and raised $26,000 for the Salem and Bedford clinics. Another of the Seven Summits was in the bag—Mount Kosciuszko

During the next January I climbed in Argentina, bringing in $14,000 more for Salem and Bedford. Alas, in Argentina exactly 53 weeks (yes 53 weeks again) after success in Australia, I stopped my climb for all the right reasons at 21,063 feet, a little short of the Argentine summit—the highest in the world outside of the Himalaya. Undaunted, during the summer of 2012, I went to Mount Rainier near Seattle to train for the other two Seven Summits, in Antarctica and Alaska.

A fall of grace at Mount Rainier led to a diagnosis of three aneurysms in three separate body systems at the same time—a medical rarity, my doctors told me. The aneurysm on my aortic arch required immediate open heart surgery. The ones each in my stomach and my intestine stayed small and didn't require intervention. My open heart surgery was a huge success. Thank you Yahweh Rophe, God Who Heals me. Heart disease and aneurysms had claimed my dad at 57 and my brother at 48. After recovering from surgery I returned to Rainier the following June for a re-do. After that climb, I prudently decided to give up technical mountaineering at high elevations.

With an A++ health rating from the doctors, I retired a few months after my 65th birthday and continued serving as an advocate in the fight against youth obesity by raising money for scholarships to our clinics. I did this by re-imagining my quest. After surrendering technical climbing, I went to Spain for a 490 mile 40-day pilgrim's walk across the continent in the autumn of 2014.

During the latter months of 2015, I sadly learned that our clinics would be closing due to cost-cutting staff concerns, just as Lori experienced at Peyton Manning Children's Hospital. Wishing to continue challenging adventures—and also wanting to continue advocating for children's wellness, I re-imagined the quest yet again. My prayers and discernment, coupled with recent news, led me to conclude: Now was the time to bring the fund-raising to my own community of Columbus, Indiana.

I moved to Columbus in 1972 and have always felt privileged and proud to call this extraordinary community home. I asked myself, "How can I help children in this city?" The answer is under consideration as I complete this book. I do know that about 200 kids learned wellness behaviors from the $130,000 raised for southern Indiana St. Vincent hospitals.

The Scope of Childhood Obesity

I know it is absolutely necessary for overweight kids to have coaching for health and behavioral management based on exercise and nutrition. Otherwise, unhealthy choices will continue producing heavy kids who become overweight adults. The co-morbidities these young people suffer as they age will grow into lifelong physical and emotional problems. Overweight adults often become an economic drain to their communities, because work place attendance and performance suffer from unhealthy heavy people unable to do their jobs. Medical costs escalate as the quality of life declines—an avoidable circumstance that will plague 21st century society.

Coaching children to eat well and to exercise is as basic as teaching them to read, do math and science, operate electronic devices—and pray. As I experienced with my Aunt Angie, each child deserves an advocate who demonstrates and encourages exercise and healthy eating. We all benefit from inspiration. Along with raising funds, I hope my treks will inspire people of all ages to become more active. As one woman told me, *"I know I don't look like I lost 20 pounds, but I have. I read about you in the paper and then I heard you speak. I'm no kid, but I can change my behavior too. My doctor is very impressed. I feel better. I am getting stronger. And my adult kids, their spouses, and my grandchildren have noticed. Thank you."*

Such words inspire me to continue trekking, raising money, and fighting obesity.

What's Next?

"**B**ut what's up next?" is a question I still get from kindly people who recognize me and from strangers who know my story from the news media. Lori and I believe our next project will be the Grand Canyon rim-to-rim descent to Phantom Ranch and ascent, probably in autumn, 2016. Meantime, I continue to train and sustain. I walk, bicycle, or play tennis 120 minutes virtually every day

Yet another project has consumed me since returning from Camino in Spain in October, 2014. This publishing adventure incorporates one of my first loves: writing. Using my journals, I completed this book to tell the story behind my quest to reach the Seven Summits while helping others. I have collected wonderful stories from each of the mountains, their countries, the people I met, and how each of these things spiritually touched my life.

All of this has happened because others saw in me what I didn't see in myself—a story waiting to be told. My "encouragers" (the translation of Barnabas' name in the New Testament) were inspired by these stories. I hope you are will also be encouraged and inspired. More stories are waiting to be told.

In Appreciation

I want to thank Rabbi Arnold for his beautiful Jewish prayer for travel. I recited it every morning, Arnold. On Summit Night and Day, I recited the prayer later in the day, while back at camp, in joyful thanksgiving for getting up and down Kili. Thanks, Arnold, to you and your temple congregation for their support. It was awesome knowing Trek for Kids had interfaith spiritual and financial support.

I appreciate Dick and the senior community at Franklin United Methodist Home, who were praying for me. Likewise, Phyllis and Baptist Homes of Indiana. Ditto to Mike and the Men's Ministry at St. Bartholomew; students and teachers from St. Mary's; Tim and Jennings High School; and Floyd and Jennings Middle School. Also thanks to Angee and the First Christian Church and much appreciation to Connie for the prayers and pennies from New Bethel and Alert United Methodist. And a hearty thank you to all my supporters at St. Vincent Jennings.

I am so grateful for Godlisten and his Zara company. God-y you are so awesome!

To the Virgin Health Miles Team, thank you for your lead support. When I put my Go Zone pedometer on, it's done mindfully of an organization that, like Godlisten, knows the value of partnership. Thank you VHM also for your inaugural "Eye on Wellness Award." I am humbled and gratified.

Again, so many, many of you prayed, as I asked, for the summit climb. Thank you for your prayers. I felt them as I basked in that sunrise glow on Uhuru Peak ... the below zero mercury temp jumped up several degrees ... even thawed my frozen water!

God bless you.

About the Author

Wally at Gorak Shep.

Since turning age 59 in 2007, Walter Glover has climbed on five of the Seven Summits, the highest mountains on each of the seven continents. He climbed on Mount Rainier twice and trekked along the 490 mile pilgrimage across Spain—The Way of St. James, El Camino. A pastoral care hospital chaplain, Walter's expeditions raised $130,000 to fight childhood obesity in southern Indiana.

The quest was for all the Seven Summits, but that dream was re-imagined after a fall on Mount Rainier showed Walter suffered from three aneurysms in three separate body systems, a medical rarity. One of the aneurysms required open heart surgery.

Glover retired from St. Vincent Hospitals in southern Indiana at age 65. The father of two and grandfather of two, he makes his home in Columbus, Indiana, with life partner Lori Walton, a registered nurse and certified health coach who helped start the weight management clinics for overweight children at his three hospitals.

Glover has worked as a professional, award-winning journalist and also holds a Master's Degree in Theologic Studies from St. Meinrad Seminary. He is a certified grief counselor. When not on expedition, his retirement activities include providing bereavement support to three groups, including bereft parents.

These compelling stories from the mountains are told from the perspective of a wellness advocate, senior citizen, world traveler, heart surgery survivor, theologian, grief counselor, adventurer, mountaineer, and family man.

CPSIA information can be obtained
at www.ICGtesting.com
Printed in the USA
FFOW03n1943160116
20411FF